Multicultural Music

Lyrics to Familiar Melodies and Authentic Songs

By
Connie Walters

Cover and Inside Page Illustrations By
Diane Totten

Publishers
T.S. Denison & Company, Inc.
Minneapolis, Minnesota 55431

DEDICATION

This book is dedicated to my parents, Julius and Josephine Wojcik whose love of their Polish ancestry and traditions instilled in me a deep pride and appreciation for my heritage and a sincere respect for the heritage of all people.

ACKNOWLEDGMENTS

My sincere appreciation to my husband, children, family members, and friends for their continual help, support, and encouragement. A special thank you to Diane Totten, Ruth Tregonning, Molly McDonough, Amy Johnson, Carol Salesky, Julie Lucke, Jasmine Marie Kee, Jim and Scott O'Leary.

There are many people whose knowledge of the various countries, people, languages, and cultures was invaluable in writing this book. Most of them came from, lived in, or are presently living in the following countries.

Thank you to the following people:
Australia: Skip Reichenberger, Chris Earhart, Julie McLennan
Canada: Elli Barron, Annie and Candice Middlebrook
France: Annie and Candice Middlebrook
Japan: Harumi Czerwinski, Chieko Nakajima, Emi Nakashima, Steve and Ann Nehez
Kenya: Dr. Clement Oniang'o, Richard and Andrea Kaitany
Mexico: Phyllis Arango, Sally Guerra, Denise O'Leary
Netherlands: Marian Mathes, Marie Schlepers, William and Cecilia Wittenberg
Poland: Julius and Josephine Wojcik, Wieslaw and Zosia Winnicki, Chris and Anna Winnicki, Ziggy Kurzawa

Many thanks to the following librarians for their assistance in research:
Ron Loyd, Northfield Library; Vicky Loyd, Bob and Pat Waters, Hamburg Library; Sherry Roberts, Betsy Baier, Paula Schaffner, Ann Arbor Library; Marilyn Brown, Herrick Library; Marilyn Kwik, Hamtramck Library; and Traverse City Library.

My gratitude to the following women for their book recommendations:
Kathleen Baxter, president, Children's Small Press Collection, Ann Arbor, Michigan
Francine Levine, president, Olive Press, West Bloomfield, Michigan
Carolyn Sapsford, president, Parent-Child Fun Co., Saline, Michigan

TABLE OF CONTENTS

CONTENTS continued

INTRODUCTION

Multicultural Music offers teachers an opportunity to promote cultural awareness. Singing songs about inhabitants of various countries, learning words in their languages, and cooking and tasting the foods they eat are a few ways in which we can acquaint ourselves with the many peoples of varied cultures. In addition, we can read books about them and do crafts and projects to simulate their activities. *Multicultural Music* contains songs about eight countries, their inhabitants, and specific traditions, customs or events. There are songs that teach a few words and the numerals in each country's official language. You will also find authentic songs and recipes as well as recommended books to read and activities to do. Illustrations and patterns are provided for many of the projects.

Singing songs is a wonderful way to learn about the people of other nations. A unique feature of *Multicultural Music* is the use of songs written to popular melodies as a method of teaching. Singing is a successful tool for learning. It is fun and students request that songs be sung again. They often repeat classroom songs when they are away from the school setting. Popular melodies make learning easier for the teacher and student. When singing the lyrics, be aware that the number of syllables in a line does not always match the exact number of notes in a melody. You may need to add or subtract notes to accommodate the words. Before you begin, gather materials that will enhance the learning of the songs, such as chopsticks or a sombrero. Review the pronunciations and meanings of the words. Pronunciations, translations, and definitions can be found at the beginning of the chapters in alphabetical order.

Patterns and illustrations are provided as visual aids for some songs. The teacher is encouraged to use both the auditory and visual senses as a means to teach the songs. Research shows that using more than one sense reinforces learning.

Suggestions for using the patterns are:
  • Protect the pieces with laminating film or contact paper; they will last longer.
  • Attach pellon, sandpaper, or felt tape on the back of each piece for use on the flannel board.
  • Attach magnetic tape on the back of each piece for use on the magnetic board.
  • Store in a large envelope, plastic bag, or manila folder; include the song with the pieces.

Besides the fun songs, delightful illustrations, and tasty recipes, *Multicultural Music* includes games, dance instructions, puppet making, an original story/song, flannel board activities, and ideas for festival celebrations. The students will have fun learning about people of the world. This knowledge and this awareness increase our chances of understanding and appreciating one another. As they say in Kenya, "Harambee!" Let us pull together. Have fun and enjoy!

Australia

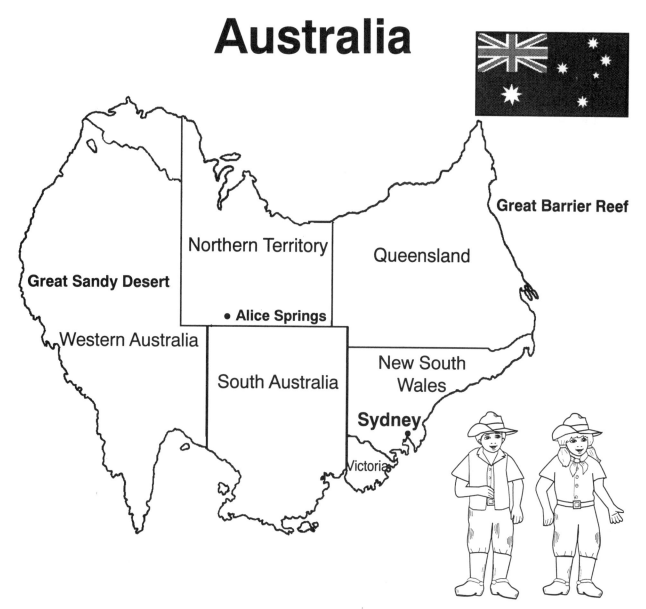

Australia is an island, a country, and a continent. Geographically, it is earth's oldest land formation. It is called the "land down under" because it is south of the equator. It receives the least rainfall of any inhabited country. More than one-half of the Australian population live in cities along the east and south coasts. Australia consists of five mainland states, one island state and two territories. It has the largest coral reef in the world. It is one of the larger exporters of agricultural products and leads in sheep-raising. Many animals are uniquely native to Australia. This is because animal life developed independently when the bridge of land that once connected Australia to Asia disappeared approximately fifty million years ago. Australia's best known tree is the eucalyptus, also known as the gum tree. There are five hundred types of gum trees in Australia. The acacia is another popular tree or shrub which grows in all regions of the country except the driest deserts. Australia's first settlers discovered that they could weave acacia into fences, roofs, and framework for the mud-plastered walls of their dwellings. They used the term "wattling" instead of "weaving" and the acacia became known as the wattle. Wattle Day is celebrated in December when the trees begin to blossom.

WORD LIST

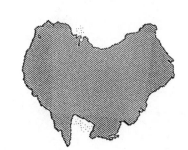

Translations

billy   a can for outdoor cooking and boiling water

billy tea   tea made in a billy over an open fire in the bush

bloke   a man

cobber   a friend

dinkum   It's true!; genuine

jackeroo   a ranch worker

mate   a close friend

outback   the Australian back country; the region remote from urban areas and inland from the coast; the interior

paddock   a meadow

station   sheep or cattle ranch

DEFINITIONS

billabong: a backwater caused by overflow from a river and forming a stagnant pool; a stream bed usually dry but filled seasonally

blue gum tree: a eucalyptus tree

cassowary: a large Australian bird similar to an ostrich but smaller; it runs swiftly but cannot fly

coral: a stony, often brightly colored substance consisting of certain kinds of skeletons of tiny sea animals

crocodile: a large reptile with a long body like a lizard but much larger

dingo: a wolf-like wild dog of Australia that feeds chiefly on wallabies and sheep

emu: a very large Australian bird that cannot fly; it has long sturdy legs and runs very fast

eucalyptus: a group of very tall evergreen trees that grow in Australia

Australian Great Barrier Reef: a chain of coral reefs and coral islands; the largest deposit of coral in the world, located along the northeastern coast of Australia

joey: a young kangaroo

kangaroo: a mammal with very strong hind legs which give it great leaping power, a heavy tail which gives it both balance and support, and small forelegs

koala: a gray furry mammal of Australia that has large ears and no tail and looks like a small bear; it lives in trees and feeds on the leaves of eucalyptus trees

kookaburra: an Australian bird which has a loud braying call that sounds like a laugh

platypus: an egg-laying mammal of Australia with webbed feet, a bill like a duck, and a tail like a beaver

thorny lizard: a lizard in the deserts of central and southern Australia that is just like the horned toad; it eats ants

wallaby: any one of various small or medium-sized kangaroos; some wallabies are no larger than rabbits

wattle: one of 600 types of flowering trees that can be found throughout Australia

wombat: a burrowing marsupial that is found only in Australia

Australia is the world's largest island and smallest continent. Places to see are beautiful cities such as Adelaide, the state capital, the bush with its unique animals, the outback where families live on outstations miles apart, and the Great Barrier Reef which is actually a chain of 2,600 coral reefs and 320 coral islands.

AUSTRALIA
(Melody: Pop Goes the Weasel)

Around and around in the ocean I go
Australia is an island
The smallest continent in the whole world
A country that's an island.

A SONG ABOUT AUSTRALIA
(Melody: Pick A Bale of Cotton)

Australia—has the most marsupials
Australia—has eucalyptus trees

Australia—fish hide in the Barrier Reef
Australia—it's in the Coral Sea

Australia—listen to the kookaburra
Australia—laughing in the tree

Australia—emu's at the billabong
Australia—with the wallaby

Australia—swimming in December
Australia—in June you winter ski.

> **Word List:** *marsupial, eucalyptus, Barrier Reef, Coral Sea, kookaburra, emu, billabong, wallaby*

Australians speak English but they also have a vocabulary of their own.

SAY IT AGAIN
(Melody: Going To Kentucky)

Now, a friend is a cobber
A close friend is a mate
A man is a bloke
Isn't that just great!

A ranch is a station
Rancher's—a jackeroo
A meadow is a paddock
Dinkum means it's true!
(repeat)

> **Word List:** *cobber, mate, bloke, station, jackeroo, paddock, dinkum*

COME WITH ME
(Melody: Band of Angels)

Come with me and see
The outback in Australia
The outback in Australia
The outback in Australia
Come with me and see
The outback in Australia
That's where I want to be.

I see one, I see two
I see three little dingoes
I see four, I see five
I see six little dingoes
I see seven, I see eight
I see nine little dingoes
Ten little dingoes I see.

Now, come with me and see
A station in Australia
A station in Australia
A station in Australia
Come with me and see
A station in Australia
That's where I want to be.

I see one, I see two
I see three flocks of sheep
I see four, I see five
I see six flocks of sheep
I see seven, I see eight
I see nine flocks of sheep
Ten flocks of sheep I see.
Now, come with me and see

The Great Reef in Australia
The Great Reef in Australia
The Great Reef in Australia
Come with me and see
The Great Reef in Australia
That's where I want to be.

I see one, I see two
I see three kinds of coral
I see four, I see five
I see six kinds of coral
I see seven, I see eight
I see nine kinds of coral
Ten kinds of coral I see.

Come with me and see
The forests in Australia
Forests in Australia
Forests in Australia
Come with me and see
The forests in Australia
That's where I want to be.

I see one, I see two
I see three kinds of wattles
I see four, I see five
I see six kinds of wattles
I see seven, I see eight
I see nine kinds of wattles
Ten kinds of wattles I see.

> **Word List:** *outback, dingo, station, Great Reef, coral, wattle*

Divide the group into two sections for a question and answer style of singing. The answer can be given by a group, a child, or a puppet.

A WEEK IN AUSTRALIA
(Melody: Twelve Days Of Christmas)

On Monday in Australia,
What do you think you'll see?
A koala in the eucalyptus tree.

On Tuesday in Australia,
What do you think you'll see?
Two wombats
And a koala in the eucalyptus tree.

On Wednesday in Australia,
What do you think you'll see?
Three platypus
Two wombats
And a koala in the eucalyptus tree.

On Thursday in Australia,
What do you think you'll see?
Four crocodile
Three platypus
Two wombats
And a koala in the eucalyptus tree.

On Friday in Australia,
What do you think you'll see?
Five kangaroo
Four crocodile
Three platypus
Two wombats
And a koala in the eucalyptus tree.

On Saturday in Australia,
What do you think you'll see?
Six cassowaries
Five kangaroo
Four crocodile
Three platypus
Two wombats
And a koala in the eucalyptus tree.

On Sunday in Australia,
What do you think you'll see?
Seven thorny lizards
Six cassowaries
Five kangaroo
Four crocodile
Three platypus
Two wombats
And a koala in the eucalyptus tree.

Word List: koala, eucalyptus, wombat, platypus, crocodile, kangaroo, cassowary, thorny lizard

The kookaburra, sometimes called the laughing jackass, is a noisy bird of the Australian forests. A large kookaburra measures approximately eighteen inches and has a four-inch bill. It is a member of the kingfisher family but does not eat fish. It eats large insects, small reptiles, and amphibians. The cry of the kookaburra resembles human laughter. In Australia, it is known as the bushman's clock because its cry can be heard at dawn and at dusk.

KOOKABURRA
(Melody: Boom, Boom, Ain't It Great To Be Crazy?)

Oh, up in the eucalyptus tree
Kookaburra laughed so heartily
Koala jumped when she heard that laugh
Fell from the tree on a big wombat.

Refrain:
Ha-ha! Everything is funny
Ha-ha! Everything is funny
Kookaburra laughs in the blue gum tree
Ha-ha! Everything is funny.

Oh, up in the eucalyptus tree
Kookaburra laughed so heartily
The emu ran when he heard that laugh
Slipped and he fell right on his back.

Refrain:
Ha-ha! Everything is funny
Ha-ha! Everything is funny
Kookaburra laughs in the blue gum tree
Ha-ha! Everything is funny.

Oh, up in the eucalyptus tree
Kookaburra laughed so heartily
Crocodile snapped when he heard that laugh
Bit so hard that his teeth were cracked!

Refrain:
Ha-ha! Everything is funny
Ha-ha! Everything is funny
Kookaburra laughs in the blue gum tree
Ha-ha! Everything is funny.

Word List: eucalyptus, kookaburra, koala, wombat, blue gum tree, emu, crocodile

The birds and mammals in these two songs are native to Australia. The kangaroo, wallaby, koala, wombat, and the brush-tailed possum are animals that belong to the marsupial species. One characteristic is that the female carries her young in her pouch. The platypus, sometimes called a duck mole, is an egg-laying mammal. The emu and the cassowary are flightless birds.

STRANGE ANIMALS
(Melody: Reuben and Rachel)

See the big bird with the long legs
It can run but it can't fly
Tiny wings hide in its feathers
Emu is an Australian bird.

What's that big and furry animal
With a joey in her pouch?
She is hopping in the grassland
I know she's a kangaroo.

See that furry duckbill animal
With web feet and paddle tail
He looks like a duck and beaver
He is called a platypus.

What's the animal in the gum tree
Eating leaves and buds all day?
She looks like a sleepy teddy
They call her a koala bear.

Word List: *emu, joey, kangaroo, platypus, koala*

ACTION SONG
(Melody: Bluebird)

Emu, emu, run so slowly
Emu, emu, run so quickly
Emu, emu, faster, faster
Stop! Emu, you can rest now!

Wombat, wombat, dig so slowly
Wombat, wombat, dig so quickly
Wombat, wombat, faster, faster
Stop! Wombat, you can rest now!

Wallaby, wallaby, hop so slowly
Wallaby, wallaby, hop so quickly
Wallaby, wallaby, faster, faster
Stop! Wallaby, you can rest now!

Koala, koala, eat so slowly
Koala, koala, eat so quickly
Koala, koala, faster, faster
Stop! Koala, you can rest now!

Word list: *emu, wombat, wallaby, koala*

Billabong—a watering hole

THE BILLABONG SONG
(Melody: It Ain't Gonna Rain No More)

Oh, I'm looking for the billabong
Oh, where is the billabong?
I'm really hot; my throat's so dry
Where is that billabong?

Oh, billabong, billabong, billabong, bye
Billabong, billabong, bee
I've been looking for water all day
Hot and thirsty—that's me!

My horse is dry—he's moving slow
The sun's so hot and strong
He hasn't found any water yet
Where is that billabong?

Oh, billabong, billabong, billabong, bye
Billabong, billabong, bee
We've been looking for water all day
Hot and thirsty are we!

The wallaby and kangaroo
They're just hopping along
They haven't found any water yet
Where is that billabong?

Oh, billabong, billabong, billabong, bye
Billabong, billabong, bee
We've been looking for water all day
Hot and thirsty are we!

The cassowary's running fast
The emu's running strong
I think they see some water ahead
Is it that billabong?

Oh, billabong, billabong, billabong, bye
Billabong, billabong, bee
We've been looking for water all day
Hot and thirsty are we!

Oh, we're heading for that billabong
Yes, we're moving right along
I'll be making billy tea
And singing my favorite song.

Oh, billabong, billabong, billabong, bye
Billabong, billabong, bee
We've been looking for water all day
Hot and thirsty are we!

KOOKABURRA

Kook - a - bur - ra sits on an old gum tree,——

Mer - ry, - Mer - ry, King of the bush is he,—— Laugh, Kook- a - bur - ra,

Laugh, Kook - a - bur - ra, Gay your life must be.

The kookaburra pattern can be made into a stick puppet.

WALTZING MATILDA
(This nineteenth-century ballad has become Australia's unofficial national song.)

3. Up rode the squatter, mounted on his thoroughbred,
Down came the troopers, one, two, three:
"Where's that jolly jumbuck you've got in your tucker bag?
You'll come a-waltzing Matilda with me."

Chorus:
Waltzing Matilda, Waltzing Matilda,
You'll come a-waltzing Matilda with me.
"Where's that jolly jumbuck you've got in your tucker bag?
You'll come a-waltzing Matilda with me."

4. Up jumped the swagman, sprang into the billabong.
"You'll never catch me alive," said he.
And his ghost may be heard as you pass by that billabong.
"You'll come a-waltzing Matilda with me."

Chorus:
Waltzing Matilda, Waltzing Matilda,
You'll come a-waltzing Matilda with me.
And his ghost may be heard as you pass by that billabong,
"You'll come a-waltzing Matilda with me."

         TSD 02267-8 • *Multicultural Music*

WITH MY SWAG ALL ON MY SHOULDER

When first I left old Ire - land's shore, the yarns that we were told. Of

how the folks in far Aus - tra - li - a could pick up lumps of gold!

How gold dust lay in all the streets and mi - ner's right was free! 'Hur-
Chorus: With my swag all on my shoul - der, Black bil - ly in my hand. I'll

rah!' I told my lov - ing friends 'That's just the place for me.'
travle the bush-es of Aus - tra - li - a like a true born I - rish man.

Repeat for Chorus.

2. When first we reached Port Melbourne
      we were all prepared to slip,
    And bar the captain and the mate,
      all hands abandoned ship.
    And all the girls of Melbourne town
      threw up their arms with joy,
    Hurrooing and exclaiming,
      'Here comes my Irish boy!'

    Chorus:
    With his swag all on his shoulder,
    Black billy in his hand,
    He'll travel the bushes of Australia
    Like a trueborn Irishman.

3. We made our way into Geelong,
      then north to Ballarat,
    When some of us grew mighty thin,
      and some grew sleek and fat.
    Some tried their luck at Bendigo
      and some at Fiery Creek;
    I made my fortune in a day
      and *blued* it in a week!

Chorus:
With my swag all on my shoulder,
Black billy in my hand,
I'll travel the bushes of Australia
Like a trueborn Irishman.

4. For many years I wandered 'round
      to each new field about,
    And made and spent full many a pound
      'til alluvial petered out.
    And then for any job of work
      I was prepared to try,
    But now I've found the tucker track,
      I'll stay there 'til I die.

Chorus:
With my swag all on my shoulder,
Black billy in my hand,
I'll travel the bushes of Australia
Like a trueborn Irishman.

AUSTRALIAN RECIPES

Anzac Biscuits

Ingredients:

1 cup rolled oats, 1 cup sugar, 1 cup flour (sifted), 3/4 cup coconut, 1 Tbsp. golden syrup (Karo Light), 1 tsp. baking soda, 2 Tbsp. boiling water, 1/2 cup melted butter

1. Preheat oven to 300°.
2. Combine oats, sugar, coconut, and flour.
3. Combine syrup, baking soda, and water. While mixture is frothing, add butter and the dry ingredients, then mix well.
4. Spoon onto greased cookie sheet. Press down gently. Bake for 20 minutes or until golden brown.
5. Cool on wire cake racks.

Meat Pastries

Ingredients:

1 lb. ground pork (use hamburger if pork is not available), 1 onion (diced), 1 Tbsp. flour, pepper, 2 tsp. parsley, chopped, 1/2 cup stock, pastry for six tart pie-tins (pastry sticks are easy to use)

1. Mix ground pork, onion, flour, pepper and parsley in a saucepan. Stir and add stock.
2. Bring to a boil, continually stirring. Reduce heat and simmer for 15 minutes. Let cool.
3. Preheat oven to 425°.
4. Roll out pastry about 1/4 inch thick. Cut six circles for the tops.
5. Roll out remaining pastry and cut six larger circles for the bottoms.
6. Line the tart pans, fill with the meat, and add the pastry tops. (It helps to moisten the edges with water.)
7. Slit the tops and brush with milk.
8. Place on a cookie sheet and bake for 10 minutes. Reduce heat to 375° and bake for 15 minutes.
9. Allow to cool slightly for children.

Pavlova

Ingredients:

4 egg whites, 1 cup sugar, 1 Tbsp. cornstarch, 1 tsp. vanilla, 2 tsp. vinegar

Filling:

1 cup cream, 1 sliced banana, 1/4 cup pineapple pieces, 1/2 cup raspberries (or blueberries, etc.)

1. Preheat oven to 225°.
2. Beat egg whites until stiff, then gradually add sugar. Beat until stiff.
3. Fold in cornstarch, vanilla, and vinegar.
4. Spoon into springfoam pan and bake for 75 minutes or until firm.
5. Turn off oven, open oven door, and allow pavlova to cool while remaining in the oven.
6. One hour before serving, whip cream. Cover pavlova with half the whipped cream.
7. Cover the whipped cream with the assorted fruits. Finish top layer with remainder of the whipped cream.

Pumpkin Soup

Ingredients:

2 cloves garlic (use garlic press or chop very fine), 1 large onion, diced, 8 oz. mushrooms, sliced (optional), 4 Tbsp. butter, 29 oz. can pureed pumpkin, 1 Tbsp. curry, 4 Tbsp. honey, 5 cups vegetable stock, 1 cup heavy cream, salt and pepper to taste, 2 or 3 shakes cayenne (red) pepper

1. Sauté garlic, mushrooms, and onion in butter.
2. Add pumpkin, curry, honey, and stock. Heat until simmering, stirring frequently.
3. Add cream and heat through.
4. Add salt and peppers. Serve.

Lamingtons
   Ingredients:
      6 eggs, 2/3 cup sugar, 1/3 cup cornstarch, 1/2 cup flour, 1/2 tsp. vanilla
1. Beat eggs with electric mixer until thick and creamy (approximately 10 minutes).
2. Preheat oven to 350°.
3. Gradually beat in sugar.
4. Sift cornstarch and flour together and fold into the egg and cream mixture.
5. Spread in a greased 9" square pan. Bake for 30 minutes.
6. Cool on wire cake rack.
   Frosting:
      4 cups powdered sugar, 1/2 cup cocoa (baking), 1 1/2 Tbsp. butter, 1/2 tsp. vanilla, 2/3 cup milk,
2 cups shredded coconut
1. Sift powdered sugar and cocoa into saucepan of a double boiler.
2. Add butter, vanilla and milk. Heat over simmering water while constantly stirring.
3. When frosting is thick enough to coat, allow to cool.

Cut cooled cake into 16 pieces. Dip in frosting and toss each square in the shredded coconut. Allow to "set" on wire cake rack.

Tasmanian Apples
   Ingredients:
      2 lbs. apples, 2 Tbsp. sugar, 1 tsp. vanilla, 6 egg whites, 3/4 cup heavy cream, water
1. Peel and slice apples. Cook with a little water.
2. Add sugar and vanilla to the soft cooked apples.
3. Beat lightly and chill.
4. Beat egg whites until stiff. In another bowl, whip the cream.
5. Fold the egg whites and the whipped cream into the apples. Serve.

Damper (bread for the outback)
   Ingredients:
      3 cups self-rising flour, 3 oz. butter, 1/2 cup milk, 1/2 cup water
1. Preheat oven to 400°. Sift flour into a bowl. Cut in butter.
2. Add liquids to make a soft, sticky dough.
3. Turn dough onto lightly floured surface and knead lightly until smooth.
4. Shape into a round loaf and place on greased cookie sheet.
5. Cut a cross through the top of the loaf, brush with milk, and bake until golden brown (approximately 10 minutes).
6. Reduce oven to 350° and bake 15 minutes.
7. Serve hot with butter, honey, or jam.

Activities

1. Children can learn the five mainland states of Australia by making a simple puzzle. Give each student a copy of the Australian map (page 5) to glue onto posterboard. Instruct the children to color each state a different color. The five states should be separated by cutting out their individual shapes to complete the puzzle.

2. Use the animal pictures (pages 18-20) as visual aids for teaching the songs to the children. Color, laminate, cut apart, and place felt or magnetic tape on the back of each picture for use on the felt or magnetic board.

3. Students can make a booklet entitled: *Australian Animal Picture Dictionary.* Have children select 3–4 animals from their picture dictionary and write something about the animals they have selected.

4. Duplicate the animal picture cards (pages 18-20) for a memory match game.

5. Children can make a wall mural on a large sheet of newsprint entitled *Animals in Australia.*

6. Use visuals for singing the song *A Week in Australia.* Enlarge the pictures of the animals named in the song and paste them onto sheets of construction paper. Print the correct number from one to seven near the appropriate animal as indicated in the lyrics. The appropriate animal card should be held up each time that particular animal is sung in the song. Ask for seven volunteers.

7. Children can make an Aussie Dictionary. Provide each student with a copy of some of the Australian words (use the translations and definitions found on page 6). Have the children write the words and defintions on index cards – then staple the index cards into a small booklet. Let them design front and back covers. Instruct the children to select eight to ten Australian words and use them in sentences.

8. Students can act out their Australian skit. They may wish to create stick puppets of Australian children for the dramatization. The children's illustrations can be colored, laminated, cut out, and taped onto craft sticks for this purpose.

9. Dramatize a trek to the outback. Children can set up camp by a billabong, explore the outback, see Australian animals and birds, get lost, run out of water. They can look for the billabong while singing *The Billabong Song,* find the billabong, make billy tea, and eat damper with butter and syrup. They can end by singing *Waltzing Matilda.*

10. The didjeridoo (page 17) is a drone pipe played by the male Aborigines of northern Australia to accompany singing and dancing. Termites hollow out a 2–3 foot eucalyptus branch which has been pushed into the ground. Designs are carved into the wood. Students can make a mock didjeridoo. Ask parents to save long paper tubes. Follow the directions and illustrations.

11. The early Australian Aborigines used the boomerang, a throwing stick, for hunting. They would carve designs on the wood. Students can make a boomerang. Enlarge the pattern of the boomerang found on page 17. Students can trace the pattern on posterboard or the back of a cereal box. The illustrations provided can be colored, cut, pasted onto the boomerang, and then laminated. Original designs can be drawn with crayon, color markers, or stamped with paint.

12. The Aborigines manipulated bark-fiber string into over 400 distinct cat's cradle designs for amusement and to tell one another stories. Obtain a book of cat's cradles or string stories from your local library. Practice a few times before telling the stories to the children. Some figures in the stories are literal representations but many figures are abstract and do not bear any direct resemblance to their subjects.

13. Write or telephone for more information about Australia: Australian Information Service, c/o Australian Consulate General, 630 Fifth Avenue, 4th Floor, New York, NY 10111, Telephone (212) 245-4000 or Embassy of Australia, 1601 Massachusetts Avenue, NW, Washington, DC, 20036, Telephone (202) 797-3000.

BOOKS TO READ

Drac and the Gremlin
Allan Baillie
The illustrations by Jane Tanner, one of Australia's most outstanding illustrators makes this book a beautiful work of art.

The Dreamtime
Beverly Broadsky
Based on the Aboriginal story

Dreamtime: Aboriginal Stories
Oodgeroo
Australian Aboriginal tales

The Flying Emu and Other Australian Stories
Sally Morgan
Twenty traditional Australian Aboriginal stories

Going for Oysters
Jeanie Adams
An Australian Aboriginal family goes oystering.

Imagine
Alison Lester
Illustrations of animal in their various settings including the Australian bush

Kolah The Koala
Jon Resnick
Photographs of a koala in its natural habitat

Kylie's Concert
Patty Shehhan
A tale of a koala and her rainforest friends

Kylie's Song
Patty Shehhan
A story of a koala and her desire to do what her heart wishes

My Grandma Lived in Gooligulch
Graeme Base
A rhymed tale with beautifully illustrated Australian animals and birds

One Wooley Wombat
R. Trinca and Kerry Argent
A counting book of fourteen Australian animals

Possum Magic
Mem Fox
Grandma Possum takes baby Hush around Australia to find the magic to make Hush visible again

Rainbow Bird
Eric Maddern
An Aboriginal folktale from northern Australia

The Singing Snake
Stefen Czernecki
An Australian tale of a cheating snake who swallows a lark

Where the Forest Meets the Sea
Jeannie Baker
A young boy explores a rain forest in North Queensland, Australia

Wombat Stew
Marcia K. Vaughan
A dingo catches a wombat and decides to make stew much to the dismay of the emu, platypus, koala, and the echidna.

Didjeridoo

1. Decorate a sheet of brown wrapping paper using stencils, potato prints, markers, etc.

2. After it is dry, roll paper around a wrapping paper tube and secure with glue.

3. Have the children play the didjeridoo, similar to the kazoo, by humming into one end of the tube.

Boomerang

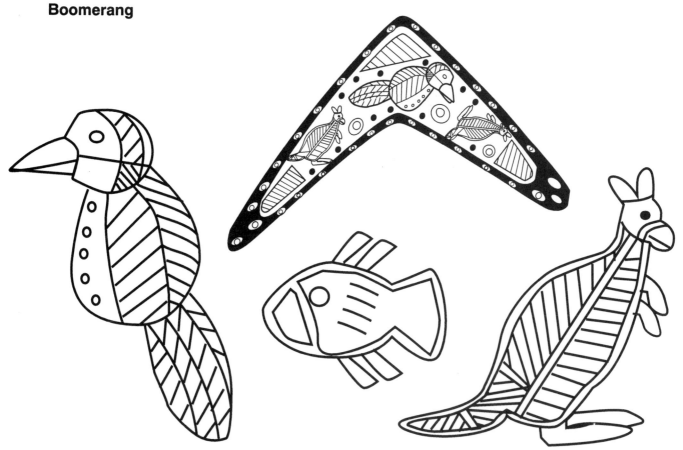

17

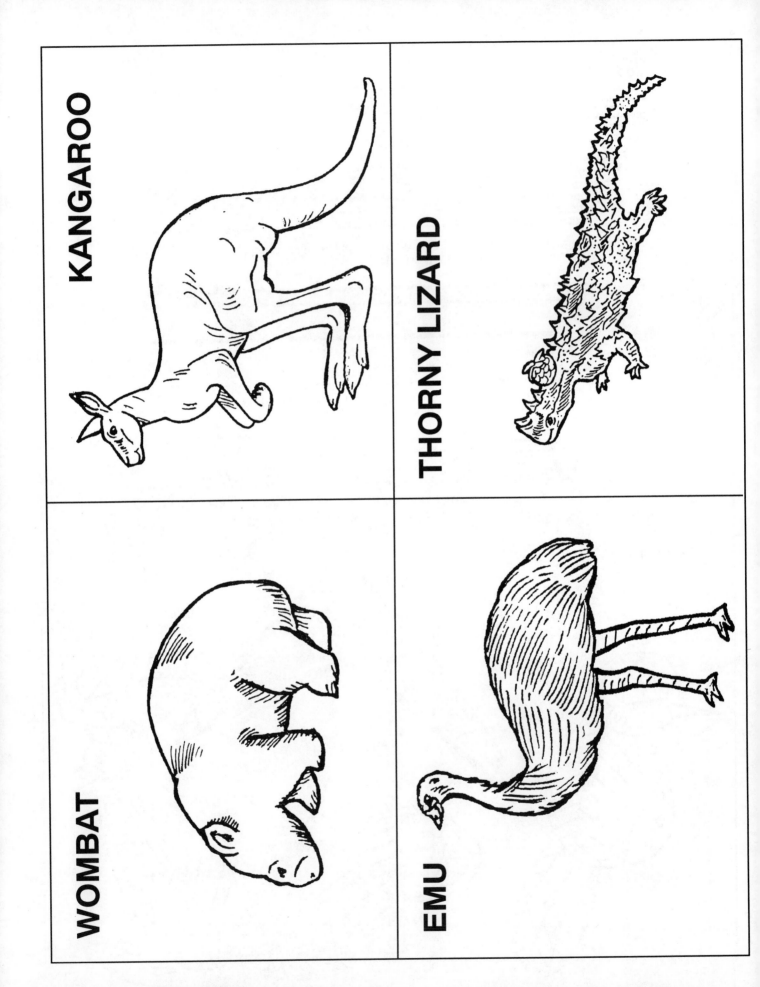

KANGAROO

THORNY LIZARD

WOMBAT

EMU

TSD 02267-8 • *Multicultural Music*

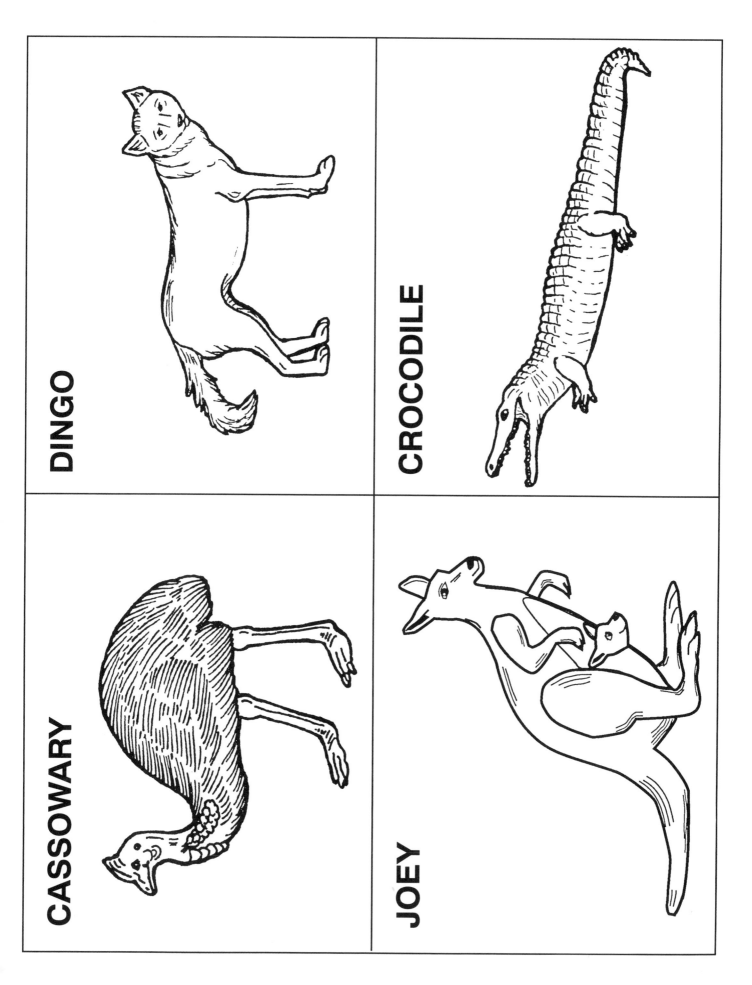

DINGO

CROCODILE

CASSOWARY

JOEY

TSD 02267-8 • *Multicultural Music*

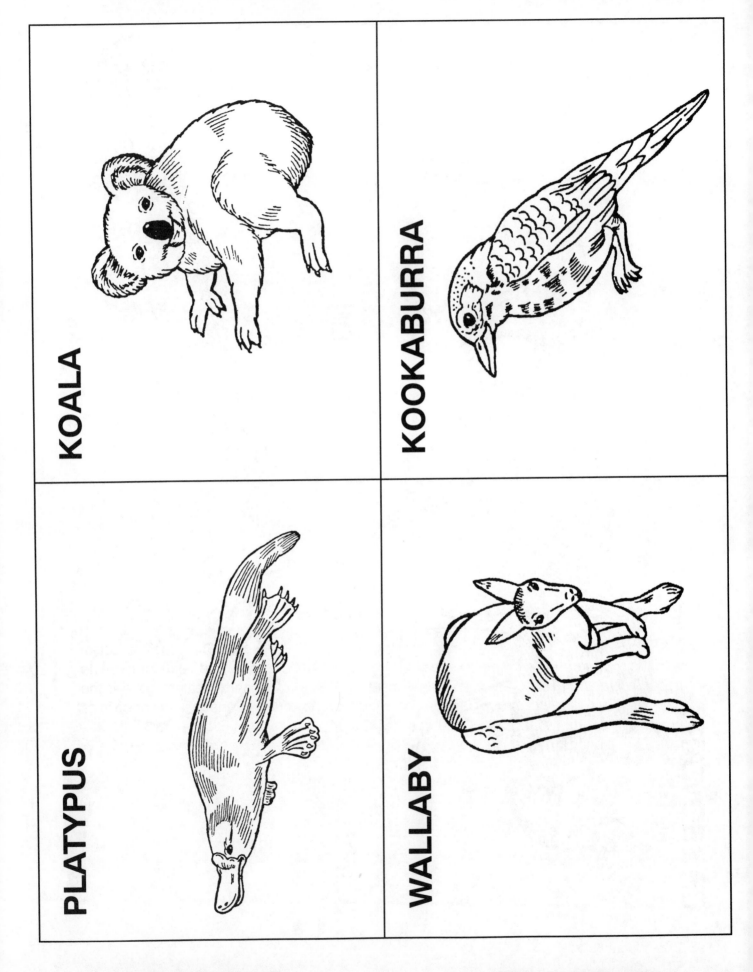

KOALA

KOOKABURRA

PLATYPUS

WALLABY

Canada

Canada is so big that it has six time zones. It is the second largest country in the world. It is comprised of ten provinces and two territories. The landscape of Canada is beautiful with its great forests, numerous lakes, prairie fields, Arctic tundra, and fields of ice. The Iroquois Indian called it "kanata" which means "village." The early settlers gave it the name Canada. The citizens in Canada come from six continents. Canada takes pride in its numerous cultures with many ethnic festivals and parades throughout the year. The native people, Indians and Inuits, are among those who proudly acclaim their heritage. Italian, German, Ukrainian, Portuguese, Dutch, Polish, Greek, and Inuktitue are among the forty languages spoken in Canada. The two official languages are English and French. Canada's national sport is ice hockey. The Montreal Canadians have been winners of the Stanley cup trophy more often than any other team in the National Hockey League. Canada has two national symbols—the maple leaf and the beaver. There are many kinds of maple trees in Canada. The maple leaf is admired for its beautiful fall colors, a reminder of the multiculturalism which is celebrated in Canada. The beaver was chosen as a national symbol because it is industrious, courageous, and persevering. These impressive qualities are symbolic of the Canadian people.

Word List

Translations

un (uhn)	one
deux (de)	two
trois (twa)	three
quatre (ka-tre)	four
cinq (sank)	five
six (sees)	six
sept (set)	seven
huit (weet)	eight
neuf (neuf)	nine
dix (dees)	ten

Pronunciation Key

ay: as in tray; **a**lien
 y: as in b**y**; l**ie**; s**igh**
ee: as in l**ea**p; pr**ie**st
 u: as in d**u**st; p**u**n
 a: as in l**ah** d**ee** d**ah**
 e: as in s**e**ven; r**e**st
 i: as in p**i**n; b**ee**r; m**i**rror
 o: as in p**o**ke; l**oa**n; r**oa**m
oo: as in l**oo**ny; s**ou**p
 j: as in **j**am; **g**iraffe
 g: as in **g**ate; a**g**ain
 s: as in **S**anta; help**s**
 z: as in **z**oo; ea**sy**

Definitions

Bonhomme: (bon-om) a lively seven-foot snowman who wears a red winter hat and sash; he is the symbol of the Québec Winter Carnival

buckets: cylindrical containers; the pioneers hung wooden buckets on nails to catch the sap flowing down the spiles inserted into maple trees

Carnaval: Carnaval de Québec, a ten-day celebration of winter which attracts more than 500,000 persons each year

hatchet: a light ax used by North American Indians as a weapon and a tool; a tomahawk

ice sculptures: beautiful sculptures such as the two-story ice palace, the Eiffel Tower, and a gingerbread house made entirely of ice which can be seen at the famous Quebec City Winter Carnival

Inuit: a word that means "people" in the Inuktitut language; original settlers of the wilderness in the Arctic Circle, often called Eskimo

Iroquois (ir-o-kwa): North American Indian tribe formerly living in Québec, Ontario, and New York State

natives: the native people of the land: in Canada and the United States this term is often applied to the Native American Indian

redcoats: a British soldier; scarlet coats were given to the first Mounties because it would show Indians and Americans that these lawmen were British

Royal Mounties: the Royal Canadian Mounted Police (RCMP); Canada's federal police force who also perform provincial and municipal police functions in some provinces and municipalities

sap: a sweet watery syrup; the watery substance that circulates through a plant and feeds it

settlers: the name given to those who settle in a new country or an undeveloped region; homesteaders

spile: a spout pushed into a hole drilled into maple trees to draw sap

sugar bush: a large number of maple trees

sugaring off: a pioneer term for gathering sap and making syrup

tap: to draw sap from trees

TEN PROVINCES—TWO TERRITORIES
(Melody: Twelve Days of Christmas)

I would like you to visit one province here with me
Québec is the one that we'll see.

I would like you to visit two provinces with me
Alberta and Québec are the two that we'll see.

I would like you to visit three provinces with me
New Brunswick, Alberta,
And Québec are the three that we'll see.

I would like you to visit four provinces with me
New Foundland, New Brunswick, Alberta,
And Québec are the four that we'll see.

I would like you to visit five provinces with me
   Ontario,
New Foundland, New Brunswick, Alberta,
And Québec are the five that we'll see.

I would like you to visit six provinces with me
Prince Edward Island, Ontario,
New Foundland, New Brunswick, Alberta,
And Québec are the six that we'll see.

I would like you to visit seven provinces with me
Nova Scotia, Prince Edward Island, Ontario,
New Foundland, New Brunswick, Alberta,
And Québec are the seven we'll see.

I would like you to visit eight provinces with me
Saskatchewan, Nova Scotia, Prince Edward Island,
   Ontario,
New Foundland, New Brunswick, Alberta,
And Québec are the eight that we'll see.

I would like you to visit nine provinces with me
Manitoba, Saskatchewan, Nova Scotia,
Prince Edward Island, Ontario,
New Foundland, New Brunswick, Alberta,
And Québec are the nine that we'll see.

I would like you to visit ten provinces with me
British Columbia, Manitoba, Saskatchewan,
Nova Scotia, Prince Edward Island, Ontario,
New Foundland, New Brunswick, Alberta.
And Québec are the ten that we'll see.

Now its time that we visit two territories
The Northwest and the Yukon we'll see.

Word List: *un, deux, trois, quatre, cinq, six, sept, huit, neuf, dix.*

Canada has two official languages: English and French. Eighty percent of the people of Quebec speak French. Ontario also has a significant French-speaking population.

JACQUES AND I
(Melody: Alouette)

I will count the numbers all in English
Jacques will count the numbers all in French.

I will say that this is one
Jacques will say that this is un
I say one; he says un.

I will count the numbers all in English
Jacques will count the numbers all in French.

I will say that this is two
He will say that this is deux
I say two; he says deux
I say one; he says un.

I will count the numbers all in English
Jacques will count the numbers all in French.

I will say this is three
Jacques will say that this is trois
I say three; he says trois
I say two; he says deux
I say one; he says un.

I will count the numbers all in English
Jacques will count the numbers all in French.

I will say that this is four
Jacques will say that this is quatre
I say four; he says quatre
I say three; he says trois
I say two; he says deux
I say one; he says un.

I will count the numbers all in English
Jacques will count the numbers all in French.

I will say that this is five
Jacques will say that this is cinq
I say four; he says quatre
I say three; he says trois
I say two; he says deux
I say one; he says un.

Word List: *Jacques, un, deux, trois, quatre, cinq*

COUNTING IN FRENCH
(Melody: The Muffin Man)

Un, deux, trois, quatre, cinq they say
It's what they say, it's what they say
Un, deux, trois, quatre, cinq they say
It's one, two, three, four, five!

Six, sept, huit, neuf, dix, they say
It's what they say, it's what they say
Six, sept, huit, neuf, dix, they say
It's six, seven, eight, nine, ten!

This song celebrates Canada's ten provinces and two territories.

ALL CANADA TO SEE
(Melody: Battle Hymn of the Republic)

We'll drive up to Newfoundland and we'll stop to catch some fish
The Grand Banks is the place for us to have a favorite dish
The cod and herring are so great; than to Saint John's we'll go
So, let's get on the road
> On the Trans-Canadian Highway
> Now and than we'll take the byway
> Stopping in the towns and cities
> All Canada to see

Prince Edward Island has the best potatoes in the land
The scallops and the oysters are also mighty grand
Green Gables in the National Park is where we'd like to go
So, let's get on the road
> On the Trans-Canadian Highway
> Now and than we'll take the byway
> Stopping in the towns and cities
> All Canada to see

In Nova Scotia, we'll take time to sail the *Bluenose II*
We'll stop to eat some lobster as we drive the Lighthouse Route
We'll listen to the bagpipes at Saint Ann's before we go
So, let's get on the road
> On the Trans-Canadian Highway
> Now and than we'll take the byway
> Stopping in the towns and cities
> All Canada to see

New Brunswick has so many forests, beautiful to see
The paper mills and lumber yards are leading industries
The Bay of Fundy is a lovely place for us to go
So, let's get on the road
> On the Trans-Canadian Highway
> Now and than we'll take the byway
> Stopping in the towns and cities
> All Canada to see

Québec is like no other place we've ever been before
We'll learn new words like "s'il vous plait, excusez-moi, bonjour"
The Citadel in Old Québec is one more place we'll go
So, let's get on the road
> On the Trans-Canadian Highway
> Now and than we'll take the byway
> Stopping in the towns and cities
> All Canada to see

Ontario is the province where we'll see the Horseshoe Falls
We'll go to plays by Shakespeare at the Stratford Festival
Toronto's CN Tower is the highest place to go
So, let's get on the road

Translation:
sil vous plait: (see voo play)
excusez-moi: (ex-koo-zay mwa)
bonjour: (bon-jeir)

              On the Trans-Canadian Highway
              Now and than we'll take the byway
              Stopping in the towns and cities
              All Canada to see

In Manitoba, we'll go to the Winnipeg Ballet
We'll plan to watch the polar bears chase seals on Hudson Bay
The International Peace Garden is one more place we'll go
So, let's get on the road

              On the Trans-Canadian Highway
              Now and than we'll take the byway
              Stopping in the towns and cities
              All Canada to see

Saskatchewan has wheat fields; they export a lot of grain
Let's travel to Regina where the Royal Mounties train
We'll canoe the Churchill River, then to Fort Walsh we can go
So, let's get on the road

              On the Trans-Canadian Highway
              Now and than we'll take the byway
              Stopping in the towns and cities
              All Canada to see

Alberta is the province where we'll climb some jagged slopes
In Calgary we'll go see the famous rodeo
Well, Jasper Park and Lake Louise are places we must go
So, let's get on the road

              On the Trans-Canadian Highway
              Now and than we'll take the byway
              Stopping in the towns and cities
              All Canada to see

We'll view the mountains and the lakes in British Columbia
We'll stop at Butchart Gardens when we're in Victoria
Vancouver has a great park; it's the place for us to go
So, let's get on the road

              On the Trans-Canadian Highway
              Now and than we'll take the byway
              Stopping in the towns and cities
              All Canada to see

To get to Dawson City to the Yukon we will fly
The Klondike is the place for us to see how gold was mined
MacBride Museum at Whitehorse is one more place we'll go
So, let's get on the road

              On the Trans-Canadian Highway
              Now and than we'll take the byway
              Stopping in the towns and cities
              All Canada to see

The Northwest Territories is the furthest on our trip
Keewatin is where we will go to visit Inuits
The capital is Yellowknife, the last place we will go
So, let's get on the road

              On the Trans-Canadian Highway
              Now and than we'll take the byway
              Stopping in the towns and cities
              All Canada to see.

The Carnaval de Québec is a world famous festival held annually in February, in Québec City. Bonhomme, a seven-foot snowman is the mascot of this ten-day celebration. As master of ceremonies, he officially opens the winter carnival, greets visitors, and hosts events and competitions.

BONHOMME
(Melody: This Old Man)

See him come
It's Bonhomme!
With a smile for everyone
He lives in the palace that's
Made of snow and ice
Come and see; it's very nice!

See him come
It's Bonhomme!
Carnival has now begun
With ice sculptures, fireworks
And two big parades
Parties, dances, lots of games!

See him come
It's Bonhomme!
He is having so much fun!
Watching hockey tournaments,
Dog sled racing, too
There's so many things to do!

See him come
It's Bonhomme!
Everywhere to see who's won
The canoe race, skating show,
And the costume ball
Carnival is fun for all!

> **Word List:** *Bonhomme, ice sculptures*

BONHOMME, HAPPY SNOWMAN (English)
(Melody: Bluebird)

Bonhomme, Bonhomme
Happy Snowman
Bonhomme, Bonhomme
Happy Snowman
Bonhomme, Bonhomme
Happy Snowman
We're very glad to see you!

BONHOMME DE NEIGE (French)
(Melody: Bluebird)

Bonhomme, Bonhomme, tu es content
(Bon-om, Bon-om, too ay con-tant)
Bonhomme, Bonhomme, tu es content
Bonhomme, Bonhomme, tu es content
Nous sommes ravi de te voir.
(Noo sum ra-vee de te vwar)

The Native people of Canada love to sing and tell stories. Many stories are tales of how things came to be, such as the creation of the world or how the turtle got its shell. This story-song tells of the discovery of maple syrup.

CHIEF WOKSIS AND THE SWEET STEW
(Melody: Good King Wenceslas)

Iroquois Chief Woksis went
Out one early morning
Pulled his hatchet from a tree
I will tell his story
The brave chief rode far away
Fast as he was able
Didn't see the gash he'd made
Deep inside the maple.

At the bottom of that tree
Was a birch-bark bowl
In it sap dripped quietly
Coming from the hole
Drop by drop the bowl was filled
Nearly to the top
His wife took the water* home
Poured it in her pot.

Brave Chief Woksis came back late
Hungry and so tired
Smelled the pot of homemade stew
Cooking on the fire
Oh, how good the stew did taste
They ate all the meat
For the water from that tree
It was maple sweet.

> **Word List:** *Iroquois, hatchet, squaw*

*When sap first drips from the sugar maple tree, it is thin in consistency and colorless. Chief Woksis's wife mistook it for water.

Interesting Facts:
- The ice palace is a two-story structure made entirely of snow and ice.
- Teams paddle small boats over and through ice floes in a famous canoe race held each year at the Québec Winter Carnival.

The maple tree is sometimes called the sugar factory. There are four maple trees that are tapped for sap: black maple, red maple, silver maple, and sugar maple. The sugar maple runs the sweetest sap.

THE SUGARING OFF SONG
(Melody: Mulberry Bush)

Let's go find a sugar bush
A sugar bush, a sugar bush
Let's go find a sugar bush
So we can tap the trees.

This is the way we drill the holes
Drill the holes, drill the holes
This is the way we drill the holes
We drill holes in the trees.

This is the way we pound the spiles
Pound the spiles, pound the spiles
This is the way we pound the spiles
We push them in the trees.

This is the way we hang the buckets
Hang the buckets, hang the buckets
This is the way we hang the buckets
We hang them on the trees.

This is the way the sap drips down
The sap drips down, the sap drips down
This is the way the sap drips down
It drips down from the trees.

This is the way we boil the sap
Boil the sap, boil the sap
This is the way we boil the sap
The sap from maple trees.

Now we have some maple syrup
Maple syrup, maple syrup
Now we have some maple syrup
Our food will be so sweet

> **Word List:** *sugaring off, sugar bush, tap, spiles, buckets, sap, maple syrup*

THE SUGAR TREE FACTORY
(Melody: Up On the Housetop)

Say would you like to go with me
To the sugar factory?
We'll tap the trees that are very sweet
Sugary sap is what we'll see.

Tap, tap, tap won't hurt the tree
Tap, tap, tap, do you agree?
The sap that we find will taste so great
We'll make some syrup for my pancake.

The Royal Canadian Mounted Police (RCMP) enforce federal laws throughout Canada and are provincial police for most of the provinces. There are more than eleven thousand men and women all across Canada wearing the uniform of the mounted police.

THE ROYAL MOUNTIES
(Melody: I've Been Working On The Railroad)

We need justice, law and order
The homesteaders cried out
The Northwest is so very lawless
The prime minister did shout
We need men to tame the wild west
Protect the settlers day and night
We can call them Royal Mounties*
They'll uphold the right.

Mounties, won't you come?
Mounties, won't you come?
Mounties, won't you come?
And help us out?
Mounties, won't you come?
Mounties, won't you come?
Mounties please come help us out.

Mounties help so very many people
Natives, Inuit, and settlers, too
When there's any problem or trouble
Mounties come to rescue you.

Just call the—
Mounties, they will help you out.
They are brave and loyal, too
'Cause they're the—
Mounties, Canada's redcoats
Men and women brave and true!

> **Word List:** *Royal Mounties, natives, Inuit, settlers, redcoats*

*North-West Mounted police was the original name given to these lawmen in 1873; it was changed to Royal Canadian Mounted Police (RCMP) in 1924.

RCMP
(Melody: Are You Sleeping)

RCMP; RCMP
You are brave; you are true
You want law and order
You want law and order
We do, too; we do, too!

RCMP; RCMP
You are fair, honest, too!
You do what is right
You do what is right
We're proud of you!
We're proud of you!

ALOUETTE
(French Canadian)

A - lou-et - te, gen - tille A - lou-et - te,

A - lou-et-te Je te plu - me - rai. *Fine* (Teacher) 1. Je te plu - me - rai la tête,

(Children) (Teacher) (Children)

Je te plu - me-rai la tête, Et la tête, et la tête Oh! *D.C. al Fine*

2. Le bec – the beak
3. Le nez – the nose

4. Le dos – the back
5. Les pattes – the feet

6. Le cou – the neck
Note: la tête – the head

TSD 02267-8 • *Multicultural Music*

IROQUOIS LULLABY
(Iroquois Indian Song)

Ho, Ho,_____ Wa - ta - nay, Ho, Ho,_____ Wa - ta - nay,

Ho, Ho,_____ Wa - ta - nay, Ki - yo - ke - na, Ki - yo - ke - na.

Sleep, sleep, little one,
Sleep, sleep, little one,
Sleep, sleep, little one,
Now go to sleep, Now go to sleep.

BLOW, YE WINDS

'Tis ad - ver - tised in Hal - i - fax, St. John and New found - land,

A hun - dred heart - y sail - ors 'Tis whal - in' they have planned_____

Oh blow ye winds in the morn - in' Oh, blow ye winds, hi - ho!

Haul a - way your run - nin' gear, And blow, boys blow.
Fah ray me doh ray te doh

2. They tell you of the clipper ships a-runnin' in and out.
   They say you'll take five hundred whales before you're
   six months out.

3. The skipper's on the quarter deck, a-squintin' at the sails
   When up above the lookout spots a mighty school of whales.

         TSD 02267-8 • *Multicultural Music*

FLUNKY JIM
(Canadian Folk Song)

2. At night when Pa comes from the field, he calls for Flunky Jim.
    He pats me on my curly head and my hat without a brim.
    He's apt to say, "Oh, Flunky Jim, your clothes in spots are small."
    But I'm going to get my new outfit with the gopher tails next fall.

    Chorus:
    Knocking around the yard, boys, knocking around the yard
    It isn't any easy job, don't fool yourself, my pard'
    My overalls are shabby and I have no shirt at all
    But I'm going to get a new outfit with my gopher tails next fall.

3. I've courted all my gopher tails, I've almost got enough
    To buy a hat, a fancy shirt, and pants that have a cuff,
    And then I'll hand my old ones down; they really are too small.
    Oh, I'll be swell when once I sell my gopher tails next fall.

    Chorus

30

O CANADA
(English and French)

O   Ca - na - da!   Our   home and na - tive   land!
O   Ca - na - da!   Ter - re   de nos aï - eux,

True   Pa - triot   love   in   all   thy sons com - mand.   With
Ton   front est   ceint   de   fleu - rons glo - ri - eux!   Car   ton

glow - ing hearts we   see   thee rise the   true north strong and   free; From
bras   sait por - ter   l'é - pé - e il   sait por - ter   la croix! Ton his -

far   and wide, O   Ca - na - da we   stand on guard   for   thee.
toire   est une é - po - pé - e des   plus bril - lants   ex   ploits.

God   keep   our   land,   Glo - rious   and   free!
Et   ta   va - leur,   de   foi   trem - pée

O   Ca - na - da,   we stand on   guard   for   thee,
Pro - té - ge - ra nos foy - ers   et   nos   droits,

O   Ca - na - da!   We stand on   guard   for   thee.
Pro - té - ge - ra nos foy - ers   et   nos   droits

TSD 02267-8 • *Multicultural Music*

Canadian Recipes

Nanaimo Bars

Ingredients:
1/2 cup butter, 1/2 cup sugar, 1/3 cup unsweetened cocoa, 1 tsp. vanilla, 1 egg (beaten), 1 cup unsweetened dried coconut, 2 cups graham cracker crumbs, 1/2 cup chopped walnuts

1. Melt butter over low heat. Add sugar, cocoa, vanilla, and egg. Cook over medium heat until thick, stirring constantly.
2. Remove from heat and add rest of ingredients. Stir.
3. Spread in greased 9" square pan and refrigerate for 1 hour.

Filling:
1/4 cup butter, 2 Tbsp. milk, 2 Tbsp. vanilla instant pudding or custard, 2 cups powdered sugar (sifted)

1. Cream butter with electric mixer.
2. Beat in remaining ingredients. (If mixture is too thick, add a little more milk.)
3. Spread over first layer and refrigerate for 45 minutes.

Topping:
4 oz. unsweetened baking chocolate, 1 Tbsp. butter

1. Melt chocolate and butter in a double boiler.
2. Spread on top of other layers and refrigerate. Before chocolate hardens, cut into 16 squares. Refrigerate for 1 hour and serve.

Nova Scotia Oat Cakes

Ingredients:
3 cups rolled oats, 3 cups flour (sifted), 1 cup brown sugar, 1 tsp. baking soda, 2 tsp. salt, 1 1/2 cups shortening, 3/4 cup cold water

1. Preheat oven to 350°. Combine dry ingredients. Cut in shortening.
2. Add water gradually, using a fork, until mixture can form a ball.
3. Roll onto lightly floured surface. When dough is approximately 1/8" thick, cut circles and place on a greased cookie sheet.
4. Bake for 15 minutes.

Chocolate Bread Pudding

Ingredients:
2 cups fresh, soft bread crumbs from homemade-style white bread, shredded with fork or in blender, 1 qt. milk, 1 Tbsp. butter, softened, 2 oz. unsweetened baking chocolate (in square form), 2/3 cup sugar, 2 eggs, lightly beaten, 1/2 tsp. vanilla extract, heavy cream.

1. Mix bread crumbs and milk in big bowl and let soak, stirring occasionally, for 30 minutes.
2. Preheat oven to 350°.
3. Melt chocolate in large saucepan. Stir frequently to prevent burning.
4. Remove from heat and add sugar.
5. Slowly add bread and milk mixture, stirring constantly.
6. Beat in eggs and vanilla.
7. Pour into greased six-cup baking dish and bake in center of oven for 2 hours, or until knife inserted comes out clean. Serve hot with heavy cream.

Toutière de Québec

Ingredients:
1 small onion, diced, 1 tsp, salt, 1/2 tsp. sage, 1 1/2 lbs. ground pork, 1/4 cup water, 2 frozen pie shells

1. Thaw pie shells. Combine all ingredients (except pie shells) in large pan and simmer for 30 minutes.
2. Preheat oven at 450°.
3. Put meat in one pie shell.
4. Remove the other shell and flatten it with rolling pin. Put on top of the meat pie and pinch together.
5. Bake for 15 minutes. Reduce heat to 350° and bake 5 minutes or until golden brown on top.

Kartoshnik (Potato Cake)
Ingredients:
 4 cups mashed potatoes, 6 eggs, 1 cup heavy cream, 1 tsp. salt
1. Preheat oven to 400°.
2. Beat eggs, cream and salt together. Add to mashed potatoes and beat again.
3. Spread in greased 8" x 12" pan and bake 30 minutes.
4. Cut in squares and serve hot with butter.

Wild Rice (from Manitoba)
Ingredients:
 1 cup wild rice, 4 cups water, 1/2 lb. mushrooms (sliced), 2 Tbsp. celery leaves, chopped, 1/2 green pepper, diced, 1 onion (chopped), 1 Tbsp. parsley (chopped), 1 Tbsp. pimento, 1 Tbsp. butter, 1/2 tsp. Italian seasoning, 1/2 cup vegetable or chicken stock, salt, pepper, thyme to taste
1. Bring washed wild rice and water to a boil in a large saucepan. Reduce heat and simmer 1 hour. Drain water.
2. Sauté in butter, the mushrooms, celery leaves, green pepper, onion, parsley, and pimento for 5 minutes. Add remaining ingredients and mix.
3. Combine rice and vegetables and heat together. Serve hot.

MAPLE SYRUP DAY PROJECTS:

Maple Walnut Pie
Ingredients:
 4 eggs, 2 cups maple syrup, 2 Tbsp. cooled melted butter, 2 tsp. cider vinegar, 1/4 cup walnuts (chopped), 9" pie shell
1. Preheat oven to 400°.
2. Beat eggs until they begin to thicken (approximately 2 - 3 minutes).
3. Slowly add syrup, beating constantly.
4. Beat in butter and vinegar.
5. Spread mixture in shell and bake in center of oven for 40 minutes or until golden brown.
6. Let cool and set.
7. Decorate with walnuts.

Maple Charlotte
Ingredients:
 1 envelope unflavored gelatin, 1/4 cup cold water, 1 cup maple syrup, 1 pt. heavy cream, chocolate lady fingers
1. Add gelatin to water.
2. Heat maple syrup.
3. Add gelatin and water to maple syrup. Stir over low heat until gelatin is completely dissolved. Let cool.
4. Whip cream and fold the whipped cream into the cooled syrup mixture.
5. Line a bowl with lady fingers, pour mixture on top, and chill thoroughly before serving.

Iced Maple Syrup Mousse
Ingredients:
 1 cup maple syrup, 4 eggs (separated), 1/2 tsp. vanilla, 1 1/4 cups heavy cream, 1/2 cup slivered almonds (toasted)
1. Beat egg yolks and syrup in the top of a double boiler over boiling water until thick.
2. Allow to cool. Add vanilla.
3. Whip cream. When cream is stiff, fold into the syrup.
4. Beat egg whites until stiff, then fold into syrup/cream mixture.
5. Pour in six-cup container and freeze.
6. Decorate with almonds and serve.

Give the students INFO cards to accompany the verses of the song, "All Canada to See." Photocopy the two pages, cut out the twelve cards, and glue them on 3" by 5" cards. Divide the INFO cards among four to six groups of students. Have each group present the information on their cards and sing the specific verses in the song that correspond.

Newfoundland became a Canadian province in 1949. Most of its inhabitants live in villages and fishing settlements near the sea. The Grand Banks is one of its richest fishing areas. Excellent cod, salmon, bluefin, tuna, herring, and flounder make Newfoundland one of the top fishing industry provinces. The industrial center and capital is Saint John's, one of the oldest communities in North America. Many festivals and events take place here. *INFO CARD*

Prince Edward Island is Canada's smallest province. It lies in the gulf of Saint Lawrence. Agriculture and fishing are two of its main industries. Its fertile soil produces its chief crop, potatoes. It is one of the leading producers of oysters, famous for their delicious flavor. An annual scallop festival is held yearly in June. The island boasts of its golf course, the Green Gables in the National Park. The white farmhouse from the story *Anne of Green Gables* stands along one of the fairways. The annual summer festival includes the production of a musical play based on this well-known book by Canadian novelist Lucy Maud Montgomery. *INFO CARD*

Nova Scotia has been nicknamed *Canada's Ocean Playground.* The province is almost entirely surrounded by water: the Gulf of Saint Lawrence, the Atlantic Ocean, and the Bay of Fundy. Its resorts and beautiful beaches attract many tourists. Cruises can be taken in the *Bluenose II,* a replica of a famous Canadian schooner. Many interesting fishing villages can be seen along the Lighthouse Route between Yarjough and Halifax. Lobster is plentiful; Nova Scotia leads the provinces in lobster production. The words *Nova Scotia* mean New Scotland. Saint Ann's holds a Gaelic festival each year where bagpipes are played and Scottish activities take place. *INFO CARD*

New Brunswick is called the *Picture Province* because of its natural beauty. Eighty-five percent of its land is covered with forests. Lumber yards and paper mills are plentiful. The leading industries manufacture paper and wood products. The Bay of Fundy is known for its high tides which produce the Reversing Falls at the mouth of Saint John's River. *INFO CARD*

Québec is Canada's largest province. It is twice as big as Texas. The people follow the traditions of France and eighty percent speak only French. *S'il vous plait* (if you please), *excusez-moi* (excuse me), and *bonjour* (good day) are words that you will hear throughout Québec. Old Québec, actually Québec City, is the oldest city in Canada and the capital of this province. A great view of Québec City can be seen from the Citadel, the oldest fort in North America. Vieux Québec, the oldest part of Québec City, was designated a world heritage site by UNESCO. *INFO CARD*

Ontario means *beautiful lake.* Its borders consist of the Saint Lawrence River, the Ottawa River, the James and Hudson Bays, and Lakes Ontario, Erie, Huron, and Superior. This province is famous for the Horseshoe Falls, one of the great natural wonders of the world. You can see Toronto, its capital, from the CN Tower, the world's tallest free-standing structure. The Stratford Festival in the town of Stratford is well-known for its production of plays by the famous English writer, William Shakespeare. *INFO CARD*

Assignment for students:
Underline the key words on the INFO CARDS that are identical to those in the song *"All Canada to See."*

Additional INFO CARDS to accompany the song "All Canada to See"

Manitoba is one of the three Prairie provinces. Thirty per cent of Canada's nickel production is supplied by Manitoba. The largest city and capital is Winnipeg, well-known because of the Royal Winnipeg Ballet. South of Churchill, Manitoba's seaport, polar bears wait for ice to form on Hudson Bay so they can hunt for seals. An international boundary consisting of rocks from Canada and the United States lies partly in Manitoba and partly in North Dakota. It is the International Peace Garden.   *INFO CARD*

Saskatchewan is the greatest wheat-growing region in North America. Its nickname, *Canada's Breadbasket* is well-earned because its farmers produce about half of Canada's wheat. The Royal Mounties' training center is located in Regina. A reconstruction of Fort Walsh, the original Mountie fort, is located in Cypress Hills. A favorite of canoeists is the Churchill river which runs across the northern part of the province. It connects lakes and streams and consists of rapids, waterfalls, and stretches of smooth water.
INFO CARD

Alberta supplies eighty percent of Canada's petroleum and ninety percent of its natural gas. Its nickname is *Sunny Alberta* because it has more hours of sunshine all year long than any other province. Along its southwestern border one can view the majestic Canadian Rockies. Banff and Jasper are two well-known national parks that provide spectacular scenery and wonderful outdoor activities. Lake Louise in Banff is one of the more popular vacation spots. The most popular event is a ten-day rodeo in Calgary called the Calgary Stampede.   *INFO CARD*

British Columbia is the only Canadian province on the Pacific Ocean. Its chief attractions are the beautiful coastal scenery, the grandiose mountains, thick forests, crystal lakes, and streams. At the lovely Butchart Gardens in Victoria, one can see beautiful blossoms and foliage. Also in Victoria is the Thunderbird Park which has the best collection of totem poles in the world. Stanley Park in Vancouver, with its forests, gardens, and picnic areas, is one of the biggest urban parks in North America. Vancouver is the biggest city. Victoria is the capital. Most inhabitants live in the Vancouver-Victoria area.
INFO CARD

The **Yukon Territory** is rocky and mountainous. Mount Logan in the southwest area is the highest peak in Canada. The southern half is covered with forests. The northern part is tundra, a treeless area with a permanently frozen subsoil. Whitehorse, the capital, is an important mining area. Tourists visit the MacBride Museum in Whitehorse to view the historical exhibits. Gold was discovered in the Klondike area in 1897. Thousands rushed to Dawson City during the Gold Rush. Dawson City continues to maintain the landmarks of this historic area.   *INFO CARD*

The **Northwest Territories** consists of five regions: Baffin, Fort Smith, Inuvik, Keewatin, and Kitikmeot. This is about one-third of Canada. The population includes Caucasians, Indians, Inuits, and metis (persons who are of mixed European and Indian descent). Many of the Inuit live in the interior of Keewatin and on Baffin. An aircraft can be hired in Yellowknife, the capital city, to take visitors to an Inuit village. Yellowknife is a mining center and the largest city in the Northwest Territories.   *INFO CARD*

Assignment for students:
Underline the key words on the INFO CARDS that are identical to those in the song *"All Canada to See."*

Activities

1. Provide the students with the map of Canada (pages 39-40). Instruct them to line up the two pages at the dotted line and tape together on the back side. Color the ten provinces and the two territories different colors.

2. Make two or three puzzles of the map of Canada (pages 39-40) for the students to put together. Tape the two pages of the map together and glue onto posterboard or have it copied onto cardstock. Color the provinces and territories twelve different colors for easier identification. Cut the map into pieces. (The Northwest Territories may need to be cut into a few pieces because of its large size; the Maritime Provinces may need to be kept together because of their small size.) Laminate and cut again close to the edge. Put the puzzles in separate envelopes and have them available to the students.

3. The INFO cards will provide students with basic information about the Canadian provinces and territories. Make the INFO cards as instructed on pages 34-35. Divide the cards among groups of students to present before the class. The cards correspond to verses in the song *All Canada to See*. Have the students highlight words on the INFO cards that match with words in corresponding verses of the song *All Canada To See*. Each group or the entire class can sing the appropriate verse after each presentation on a province or territory.

4. Have students trace the journey of the song on their maps. Assign the task of planning and mapping their own journey through Canada. They can write short papers on the places they would like to visit and the reasons for those choices.

5. Bonhomme is the very lively and friendly seven-foot snowman who serves as master of ceremonies for Québec's famous Winter Carnival. (Pattern found on page 38.) Children can make a jointed snowman that looks like Canada's Bonhomme. His arms can wave and his legs can kick rhythmically to the beat as they sing the song *Bonhomme* written to *This Old Man*. Make copies of the snowman on heavy white paper for children to cut out. For authenticity, his toque (hat) and sash should be colored red. Students match the letters on the various pieces and attach with brad fasteners. A plastic straw or dowel rod can turn him into a dancing stick puppet.

6. People come from all over the world to compete in carving snow and ice sculptures at Québec's Winter Carnival. If there is enough snow in your area, divide the students into small groups. They should design a snow sculpture before going outdoors to execute their plan. Invite the school principal to give prize ribbons to the winners for the most difficult, the funniest, and the most imaginative sculptures, with certificates given to all who participated.

7. Have a Maple Syrup Day. Make maple syrup and maple snow if possible. Serve maple treats brought in by parents. Recipes are included for a maple walnut pie or Canadian maple pie, maple charlotte and iced maple syrup mousse. Sing *Chief Woksis and the Sweet Stew*.

8. Have a pancake and maple syrup breakfast or supper. Ask for parent volunteers to work with the students in planning and executing this simple meal. Students can make paper Canadian flags as centerpieces for the table. Invite guests. For a program, students can sing *All Canada to See* interspersed with a shortened version of their reports on Canada's provinces and territories. Also sing *Chief Woksis and the Sweet Stew* and the other maple syrup songs.

9. Tell the children tales of the Royal Canadian Mounted Police. The book list has a few titles that can be inter-loaned through the library system. Sing the songs about the RCMP in this chapter.

10. There are three sets of picture cards illustrating the making of maple syrup: Native, pilgrim, and modern day people ("making syrup cards" found on pages 41-43). Make copies on cardstock. Laminate and cut apart. Use them as visual aids when telling the children the history of making maple syrup. Students can make little booklets to take home.

11. Read the lyrics to *Chief Woksis and the Sweet Stew*. Tell the story in your own words to the class or read it aloud as a poem before teaching the song.

12. *Folklorama* in Winnipeg and *Caravan* in Toronto are two of the largest multicultural festivals held annually in Canada. There are puppet shows, concerts, songfests, theatre presentations, dances, fireworks, and food samplings from up to forty ethnic groups. At the end of the school year, have a two to three-day Multicultural Festival. Students can repeat their favorite activities in this book. Ask parents to bring in an ethnic food that they had prepared during the past year. Make copies of the multicultural placemats for each child to color. Laminate them as keepsakes.

13. The Inuits are known for their soapstone carvings. Many sculptures depict animals and nature scenes that are part of their daily life. Provide each child with a bar of *Ivory* white soap and a plastic knife. They can carve an item of nature and buff it with a soft cloth or soft paper towel.

14. For more information write or telephone: Canadian Consul Library Information Center, Consulate General of Canada, 1251 Avenue of the Americas, New York, NY 10020-1175, Telephone (212) 596-1600 or Embassy of Canada, 501 Pennsylvania Avenue, NW, Washington, DC 20001, Telephone (202) 682-1740.

BOOKS TO READ

Buried in Ice
Owen Beattie and John Geiger
An expedition to chart a sea route across the frozen ocean above Canada

Canada Celebrates Multiculturalism
Bobbie Kalman
Multicultural celebrations and festivals in Canada

Canada under Siege
Pierre Berton
American attempts to seize Canada in 1813

The Capture of Detroit
Pierre Berton
The first Canadian victory in the War of 1812

How the Devil Got His Cat
Bob Barton
French Canadian folk tale

If You're Not from the Prairie
David Bouchard
A visual and poetic journey of memories on the prairie

Manitoba
Robert Taylor
The life and landscape of Manitoba

Mary of Mile 18
Ann Blades
In British Columbia, a young girl longs to keep a wolf-pup

A Prairie Nightmare
Pierre Berton
Hardship, perseverance, and dedication to a new life on Canada's prairies

Revenge of the Tribes
Pierre Berton
The Indians prevent another invasion of Canada

Royal Canadian Mounted Police
Richard L. Neuberger
One hundred and eighty pages of personal knowledge interwoven with historical data about the famous Mounted Police

Somewhere in Canada
Sara Ball
A picture book of Canadian animals coming to a pool of water to drink

The Story of Canada
Janet Lunn and Christopher Moore
Unforgettable stories of daily life, folk tales, and fascinating facts with paintings, photographs, maps, and cartoons

The Talking Cat and Other Stories of French Canada
Natalie Savage Carlson
French tales as told by Oncle Michel to friends he visits

They Sought a New World
William Kurelek
European immigration to Canada

BONHOMME

Canada

← Red

← Red

38

MAP OF CANADA

MAP OF CANADA

Trans-Canada Highway *

Baffin
Island

Atlantic
Ocean

Labrador

NEWFOUNDLAND

QUÉBEC

Gulf of
St. Lawrence

St. John's

Grand Banks

PRINCE
EDWARD
ISLAND

ONTARIO

Québec City

NEW
BRUNSWICK

NOVA
SCOTIA

Halifax

Bay of Fundy

Toronto

Stratford

*The white maple leaf is the sign
for the Trans-Canada Highway.
This road runs across Canada
from coast to coast.

Making Syrup

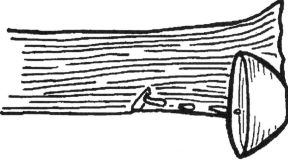

Making Syrup

NATIVE PEOPLE

Sugar month or maple moon was the name given to the few weeks when maple syrup could be made.

1. Native people cut notches into the maple's trunk with a hatchet and stuck bark or a small handcarved wooden trough into the notch.

2. A bark or wooden bowl was put on the ground to catch the sap that dripped along the trough.

3. The bowls of sap were carried to the sugar hut and placed in large hollowed-out logs; fat stones were heated and dropped into the logs to boil the sap.

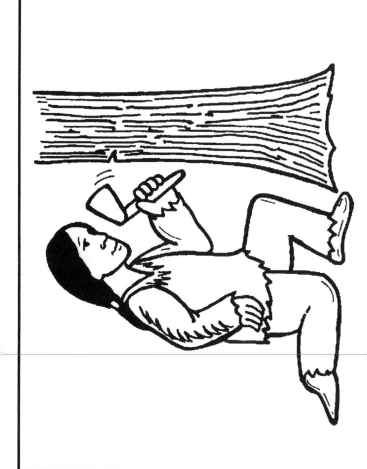

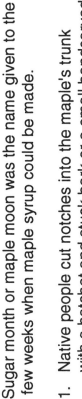

Making Syrup

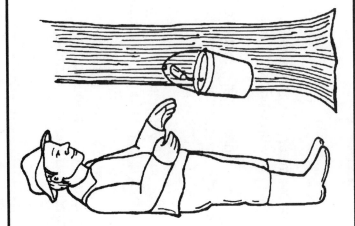

PIONEERS

The time period when maple trees could be tapped and syrup made was called sugaring off.

1. Holes were pounded into the trees and wooden spouts, called spiles, were pushed into the holes.

2. Buckets were first set on the ground and then hung on nails below the spiles.

3. The sap was poured into huge iron pots and boiled for hours over open fires.

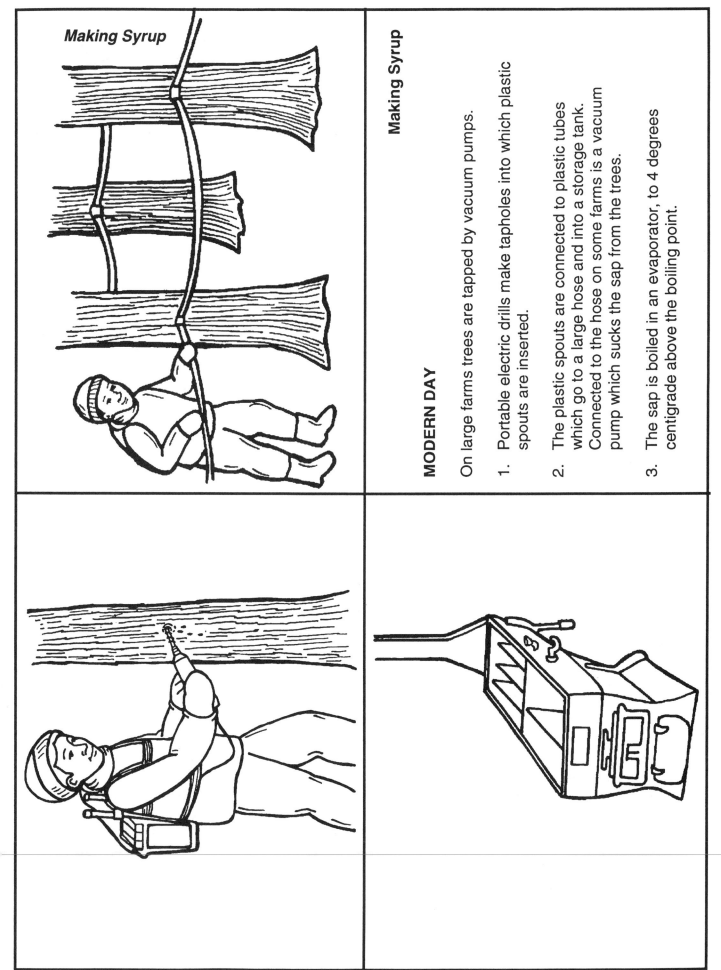

Making Syrup

Making Syrup

MODERN DAY

On large farms trees are tapped by vacuum pumps.

1. Portable electric drills make tapholes into which plastic spouts are inserted.

2. The plastic spouts are connected to plastic tubes which go to a large hose and into a storage tank. Connected to the hose on some farms is a vacuum pump which sucks the sap from the trees.

3. The sap is boiled in an evaporator, to 4 degrees centigrade above the boiling point.

France

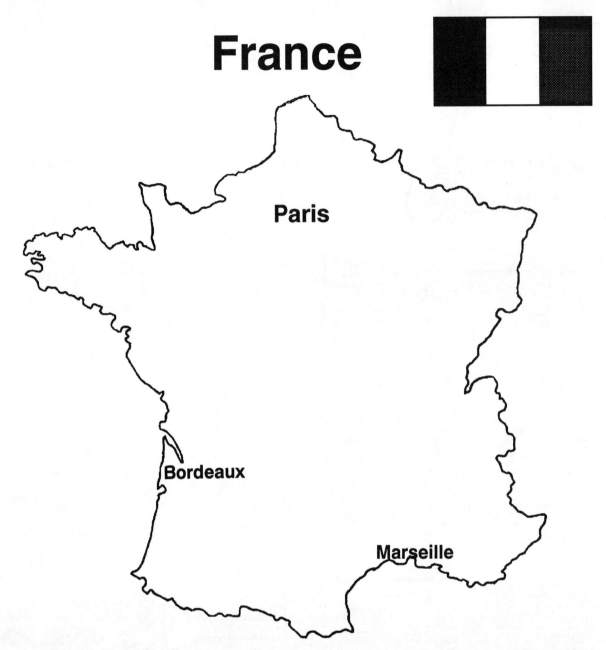

Paris

Bordeaux

Marseille

France is a beautiful, rich, historic, and powerful country. It is fifth among the countries of the world in its trade with other nations. It is shaped roughly like a hexagon with six sides. Three sides are bordered by water and three sides are mostly mountainous. Its two principle mountain chains are the Pyrenées and the Alps. Paris, the capital of France, is located on both banks of the Seine River approximately ninety miles from the river's mouth on the English Channel. It is the tourist center of France and one of the world's most important cities. Famous landmarks located in Paris are the Eiffel Tower, the Notre Dame Cathedral, the Palace of Versailles, the Louvre Museum, and the Arc de Triomphe. One-sixth of France's population lives in Paris. The French are well-known for their enjoyment of good food and good wine. Although there are several different dialects and a few other languages, French, the official language, is spoken and understood by almost the entire population. Among the notable in French history are French painters Monet, Renoir, and Pissarro; French sculptor Rodin; writers Victor Hugo and Jean-Paul Sartre; and composers Bizet, Debussy, and Gounod.

Word List

Numbers

un (uhn):	one
deux (de):	two
trois (twa):	three
quatre (ka-tre):	four
cinq (sank):	five
six (sees):	six
sept (set):	seven
huit (weet):	eight
neuf (neuf):	nine
dix (dees):	ten

Days of the Week

lundi (lun-dee):	Monday
mardi (mar-dee):	Tuesday
mercredi (mer-cre-dee):	Wednesday
jeudi (je-dee):	Thursday
vendredi (van-dre-dee):	Friday
samedi (sam-dee):	Saturday
dimanche (dee-mawnsh):	Sunday

Parts of the Body

la bouche (la boosh):	mouth
le coude (la kood):	elbow
la cuisse (la kwees):	thigh
l'épaule (lay-pal):	shoulder
la jambe (la jamb):	leg
la main (la meh):	hand
le nez (le nay):	nose
le pied (le pee-ay):	foot
la tête (la tet):	head

Pronunciation Key

ay:	as in tr**ay**; **a**lien
y:	as in b**y**; l**ie**; s**igh**
ee:	as in l**ea**p; pr**ie**st
u:	as in d**u**st; p**u**n
a:	as in l**a**h dee d**a**h
e:	as in s**e**ven; r**e**st
i:	as in p**i**n; b**ee**r; m**i**rror
o:	as in p**o**ke; l**oa**n; r**oa**m
oo:	as in l**oo**ny; s**ou**p
j:	as in **j**am; **g**iraffe
g:	as in **g**ate; a**g**ain
s:	as in **S**anta; help**s**
z:	as in **z**oo; ea**s**y

Translations:

Adieu (ad-ye):	farewell
Au revoir (o-rev-wa):	good bye
Bon appetit! (bo-na-pe-tee):	Good appetite! Enjoy your meal.
Bonjour (bon-jeir):	Good day
Bonne chance! (bon-shans):	Good luck!
Bonne nuit (bo-ne-wee):	Good night
Bonsoir (bo-ne-swar):	Good evening
café (ka-fay):	coffeehouse; informal restaurant
café au lait (ka-fay o lay):	coffee and hot milk in about equal amounts
C'est (say):	This is

C'est ça qu'on dit (say sa kon dee):   This/that is to say
C'est la vie (say la vee):   That's life!
les crêpes (lay krayp):   very thin pancakes
et (ay):   and
faire un tour (fer uhn toor):   to turn around
madame (ma-dam):   Madam (Mrs.)
magnifique (mag-nee-feek):   magnificent
merci (mer-see):   thank you
merci beaucoup (mer-see bo-koo):   thank you very much
moi (mwa):   me
mon ami (mo-na-mee):   my friend
monsieur (mise-yir):   Sir (Mr.)
le petit dejeuner (le pe-tee day-je-nay):   breakfast
Pierre (pee-er):   Peter
un, deux, trois (uhn, de, twa):   one, two, three

The Bakery

les baguettes (lay ba-get):   long, thin loaves of bread, a very popular staple in France

les biscottes (lay bee-skot):   dry toast
la boulangerie (la boo-lan-ger-ee):   bakery
les brioches (lay bree-osh):   buns
les grands pains (lay gran-pan):   large loaves of bread

The Pastry Shop

les biscuits (lay bee-skwee):   cookies
les bonbons (lay bon-bon):   candy
les croissants (lay kwa-san):   rich, crescent-shaped rolls of leavened dough
le gâteau (le ga-to):   cake
les gâteaux (lay ga-to):   cakes
la patisserie (la pa-tee-sir-ee):   shop that specifically sells pastries such as cakes, candied fruits, bonbons, croissants and quiche
les pralines (lay pra-leen):   confections made of nuts, especially almonds or pecans, stirred in boiling sugar syrup until crisp or brown

---

The Dairy

la crémerie (la crem-ir-ee):   little shop that sells only dairy products
les fromages ((lay fro-maj):   cheese
les glaces (lay glas):   ice cream
les oeufs (lay ze):   eggs
les yogourts (lay yo-gur):   yogurt

The Grocery

les **bananes** (lay ba-nan): bananas
les **carrotes** (lay ka-rot): carrots
les **cerises** (lay sir-eez): cherries
l'**épicerie** (lay pee-sir-ee): grocery store
les **pommes** (lay pom): apples

Word List for Tour de France

leader: the bicycle racer who has the fastest time in the Tour de France; he/she wears the yellow jersey

mountain king: the King of the Mountains in the Tour de France is a good climber and also possesses a strong sprint; the winner wears a white jersey with red polka dots

sprinter: a very fast and consistent bicycle rider; the winner of the sprints wears the green jersey

Tour de France: 2,500-mile bicycle race which lasts several weeks; the most popular sporting event in France

winner: the overall leader of the Tour de France who receives a golden bowl as a trophy at the end of the race

Definitions

Carmen: a very popular French opera written by Georges Bizet in 1875

les Champs-Elysées (lay shon-zay-lee-zay): the most famous thoroughfare in Paris; it leads to the Arc de Triomphe and is surrounded by very elegant shops, movie theatres and cafés

les crêpes (lay krayp): very thin pancakes made from a batter of milk, flour, and eggs

Eiffel Tower: steel structure (1,051 feet high) with large antenna at the top which transmits television and radio signals. From the top of the tower, Paris can be viewed in good weather up to a distance of fifty miles; symbolizes Paris

Guignol (gee-nyol): hand puppet; comic hero in children's puppet shows

Louvre (loov-re): originally a medieval fortress, later a palace, now one of the largest art museums in the world

le marche (le marsh): an open-air market offering fresh food for purchase

le métro (le may-tro): the Paris subway system

Opéra (o-per-a): the opera house in Paris decorated with ornate elegance and brilliant decor

Notre Dame (no-tre-dam): Gothic cathedral used as a house of worship on the Parisian island, Ile de la Cité; famous for its stained glass "Rose Window" and its gargoyles

Paris (Pa-ree): the capital of France; center of entertainment, fashion, and gourmet food

Versailles (ver-sy): one of the most magnificent royal palaces in the world; open to the public

Paris, France, is the most visited place in the world. For years it has been a world capital of art and learning. With its many famous landmarks, it attracts millions of tourists yearly.

A WONDERFUL TIME IN FRANCE
(Melody: Vive la compagnie)

Today is the day that I'm leaving for France
Come with me; come to France
We'll see the great sights
And explore this fine land
Come with me; come to France.

We'll have a wonderful, wonderful time
Go to the vineyard; eat grapes from the vine
Visit the Louvre and tour the Versailles
When we're in Paris, France.

We'll go to Jeanette's for le petit dejeuner
Come with me; come to France
We'll eat her sweet crêpes and drink café au lait
Come with me; come to France.

We'll have a wonderful, wonderful time
Go to the vineyard; eat grapes from the vine
Visit the Louvre and tour the Versailles
When we're in Paris, France.

We'll climb Eiffel Tower and see Notre Dame
Come with me; come to France
We'll listen to *Carmen* at the Opéra
Come with me; come to France.

We'll have a wonderful, wonderful time
Go to the vineyard; eat grapes from the vine
Visit the Louvre and tour the Versailles
When we're in Paris, France.

We'll ride le métro and shop at le marche
Come with me; come to France
We'll walk to the theatre; see the ballet
Come with me; come to France.

We'll have a wonderful, wonderful time
Go to the vineyard; eat grapes from the vine
Visit the Louvre and tour the Versailles
When we're in Paris, France.

We'll shop all day long on the Champs-Elysées
Come with me; come to France
We'll sit under stars at a Paris café
Come with me; come to France.

We'll have a wonderful, wonderful time
Go to the vineyard; eat grapes from the vine
Visit the Louvre and tour the Versailles
When we're in Paris, France.

DAYS OF THE WEEK
(Melody: Going to Kentucky)

I know that Monday's lundi
And mardi means it's Tuesday
It's mercredi for Wednesday
Yes, this is what they say!
I think jeudi is Thursday
Three more days to go
Vendredi is Friday
This may be all I know
Wait—Saturday is samedi
One more to recall
They say dimanche for Sunday
Hooray! I know them all!

> **Word List:** lundi, mardi, mercredi, jeudi, vendredi, samedi, dimanche

SAY IT IN FRENCH
(Melody: Rig-A-Jig-Jig) verse only

Bonjour, bonjour, c'est ça qu'on dit
Mon ami, mon ami!
Bonjour, bonjour, c'est ça qu'on dit
Good day, good day, my friend.

Bonne chance, bonne chance
C'est ça qu'on dit
Mon ami, mon ami!
Bonne chance, bonne chance
C'est ça qu'on dit
Good luck, good luck, my friend.

Merci, merci, c'est ça qu'on dit
Mon ami, mon ami!
Merci, merci, c'est ça qu'on dit
Thank you, thank you, my friend.

*Bonsoir, bonsoir, c'est ça qu'on dit
Mon ami, mon ami!
Bonsoir, bonsoir, c'est ça qu'on dit
Good night, good night, my friend.

> **Word List:** bonjour, c'est ca qu'on dit, mon ami, bonne chance, merci.

* substitute Bonsoir with Bonne nuit, Adieu, Au revoir

> **Word List:** Louvre, Versailles, Paris, le petit dejeuner, crêpes, café au lait, Eiffel Tower, Notre Dame, "Carmen'" Opéra, le métro, le marche, Champs-Elysées café

 TSD 02267-8 • Multicultural Music

The word for puppet in French is "marionette." One of the more popular puppets created in France is the heroic comic character Guignol, a hand puppet. The word for puppet show bears his name. The guignol or puppet show has been a favorite pastime in France since the mid-eighteenth century. Today, there are several well-known puppet theatres including those in Paris at the Champs-de-Mars, at the Luxembourg Gardens, and the Tuileries.

I LOVE TO COUNT
(Melody: Three Blind Mice)

Un, deux, trois; un, deux, trois,
Quatre et cinq; quatre et cinq;
I love to count in French you see
I ask you please to count with me
Un, deux, trois, quatre et cinq.

Six, sept, huit; six, sept, huit,
Neuf et dix; neuf et dix
I love to count in French you see
I ask you please to count with me
Six, sept, huit, neuf et dix.

> **Word List:** *un, deux, trois, quatre, cinq, six, sept, huit, neuf, dix*

AT THE PATISSERIE
(Melody: Kumbaya)

Un gâteau, madame
I want one
Deux gâteaux, madame
I want two
Trois gâteaux, madame
I want three
Madame, merci beaucoup!

Quatre biscuit, madame
I want four
Cinq biscuit, madame
I want five
Six biscuit, madame
I want six
Madame, merci beaucoup!

Sept croissants, madame
I want seven
Huit croissants, madame
I want eight
Neuf croissants, madame
I want nine
Madame, merci beaucoup!

> **Word List:** *patisserie, gâteau, gâteaux, biscuit, croissants, madame, monsieur, un, deux, trois, quatre, cinq, six, sept, huit, neuf, merci beaucoup.*

GUIGNOL
(Melody: Bluebird)

Guignol, Guignol, silly puppet
Guignol, Guignol, silly puppet
Guignol, Guignol, silly puppet
Oh, Guignol, you're so funny!
Guignol, Guignol, tell a story
Guignol, Guignol, tell a story
Guignol, Guignol, tell a story
Oh, Guignol, you're so funny!

Guignol, Guignol, sing a song now
Guignol, Guignol, sing a song now
Guignol, Guignol, sing a song now
Oh, Guignol, you're so funny!

> **Word List:** *Guignol*

THE THREE MARIONETTES
(Melody: Head, Shoulders, Knees, and Toes)

(Madame de Bois)
I just love to hear them sing— Magnifique!
I just love to hear them sing—Magnifique!
At the opéra they sing so sweet—la, la, la!
I just love to hear them sing—Magnifique!

(Monsieur Brioche)
I must work the whole day long—C'est la vie!
I must work the whole day long—C'est la vie!
I bake bread, croissants and les baguettes
I must work the whole day long—C'est la vie!

(Guignol)
I just want to have some fun!— Ooh la-la!
I just want to have some fun!— Ooh la-la!
Gay Pa-ree is where I want to be—Ooh la-la!
I just want to have some fun!— Ooh la-la!

> **Word List:** *magnifique, opéra, C'est la vie, croissants, les baguettes, Ooh la-la*

It is said that the French people spend a fairly good amount of their family budget on eating well. Cheese is plentiful as there is one for every day of the year (over 365 kinds). Fresh bread is a must at every meal. Grape vineyards abound throughout the countryside and wine is available everywhere.

BON APPETIT
(Melody: Fiddle-Dee-Dee)

Bon appetit! Bon appetit!
Won't you sit down and have something to eat?
This morning we went to la boulangerie
We bought les grands pains and les baguettes to eat
Bon appetit! Bon appetit!
We wish you good health and some good food to eat!

Bon appetit! Bon appetit!
Won't you sit down and have something to eat?
This morning we went to la crémerie
We bought les fromages and les oeufs to eat
Bon appetit! Bon appetit!
We wish you good health and some good food to eat!

Bon appetit! Bon appetit!
Won't you sit down and have something to eat?
This morning we went to l'épicerie
We bought les bananes et les pommes to eat
Bon appetit! Bon appetit!
We wish you good health and some good food to eat!

Bon appetit! Bon appetit!
Won't you sit down and have something to eat?
This morning we went to la patisserie
We bought les croissants and les gâteaux to eat
Bon appetit! Bon appetit!
We wish you good health and some good food to eat!

Word List: *Bon appetit!, la boulangerie, les grand pains, les baguettes, la crémerie, les fromages, les oeufs, l'épicerie, les bananes, les pommes, la patisserie, les croissants, les gâteaux*

Substitute other food items:
At la boulangerie: les biscottes, les brioches
At la crémerie: les yogourts, les glaces
At l'épicerie: les cerises, les carrotes
At la patisserie: les biscuits, les bonbons, les pralines

The Tour de France is a timed bicycle race held yearly in France. This song is about the various winners in the race. The leader wears the yellow jersey. The winner of the sprints wears the green jersey. The King of the Mountains wears a white jersey with red polka-dots. The overall winner receives a trophy.

WATCHING THE RACE
(Melody: Aiken Drum)

We'll sit along the countryside
Countryside, countryside
We'll sit along the countryside
We will watch the Tour de France

Refrain:
And we'll see them ride so very fast
Very fast, very fast
And we'll see them ride so very fast
Who will win the Tour de France?

The leader wears the yellow shirt
Yellow shirt, yellow shirt
The leader wears the yellow shirt
In the race, he is the best!

Refrain:
And we'll see them ride so very fast
Very fast, very fast
And we'll see them ride so very fast
Who will win the Tour de France?

The sprinter wears the dark green shirt
Dark green shirt, dark green shirt
The sprinter wears the dark green shirt
In the sprints, he is the best!

Refrain:
And we'll see them ride so very fast
Very fast, very fast
And we'll see them ride so very fast
Who will win the Tour de France?

The mountain king wears white with red
White with red; white with red
The mountain king wears white with red
In the mountains he's the best!

Refrain:
And we'll see them ride so very fast
Very fast, very fast
And we'll see them ride so very fast
Who will win the Tour de France?

Champs-Elysées is where it ends
Where it ends; where it ends
Champs-Elysées is where it ends
We will see who is the best!

Refrain:
And we'll see them ride so very fast
Very fast, very fast
And we'll see them ride so very fast
Who will win the Tour de France?

We'll see the winner get the prize
Get the prize; get the prize
We'll see the winner get the prize
He's the one who is the best

Refrain:
Oh, we saw him ride so very fast
Very fast, very fast
Oh, we saw him ride so very fast
And he won the Tour de France!

Many villages in France have a simple race track where children ride their bicycles and dream of becoming national heroes by winning the famous annual bicycle race, the Tour de France.

TOUR DE FRANCE
(Melody: Polly Wolly Doodle)

When Pierre was just a little lad
He would often hear his grandpa say
If you learn to ride your bike real fast
You will be the one to win the race some day.

Refrain:
Tour de France, Tour de France
Will he win the Tour de France?
Riding up and down the hills; hoping he won't have a spill
Dreaming he's the one to win the Tour de France.

Now one day, his grandpa called to him
Come and see the wonderful surprise
So Pierre ran fast. "Magnifique!" he cried
A new bike was standing there before his eyes.

Refrain

After school each day he would ride his bike
He would race so fast around the track
Then he'd pedal hard up and down some hills
And he'd ride his bike to Paris and back.

Refrain

Oh, Pierre just loved to ride and ride
He knew he had a very good chance
Cause he practiced hard and believed he could
Win the first prize in the famous Tour de France.

Refrain

Well Pierre is now a fine young man
And his dream has finally come true
For today he crossed the finish line
A great racer and a first prize winner, too!

Refrain

FRÈRE JACQUES

Translation of verse:
Are you sleeping? Are you sleeping?
Brother John, Brother John.
Morning bells are ringing. Morning bells are ringing.
Ding, ding, dong. Ding, ding, dong.

52

LES PETITES MARIONNETTES
(Little Puppets)

(Use with the puppets on page 62.)

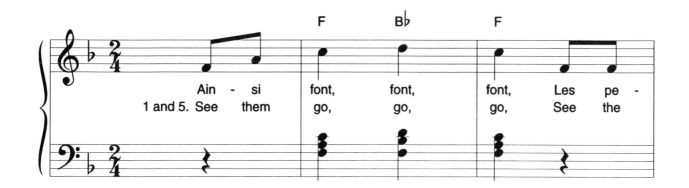

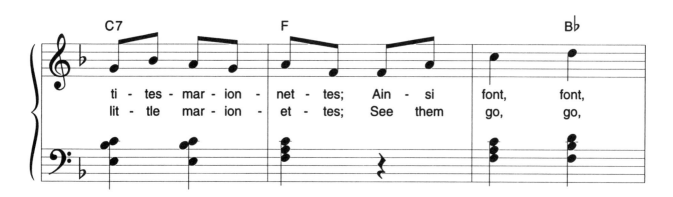

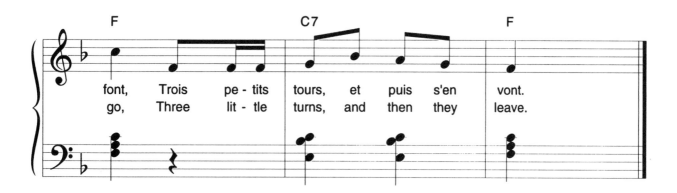

Verse 2:
See them move their heads,
See the little marionettes;
See them move their heads,
Three little nods,
    and then they leave.

Verse 3:
See them move their arms,
See the little marionettes;
See them move their arms,
Three little claps,
    and then they leave.

Verse 4:
See them move their legs,
See the little marionettes;
See them move their legs,
Three little jumps,
    and then they leave.

   TSD 02267-8 • *Multicultural Music*

SAVEZ-VOUS PLANTER LES CHOUX?

SUR LE PONT D' AVIGNON

Allegro

Sur le pont d'A - vig - non, Tout le monde y dan-se, dan-se;

Sur le pont d'A - vig - non, Tout le monde y danse en rond. Les

beaux Mes-sieurs font comme çi. Les bel - les Dames font comme ça.

Sur le pont d'A - vig - non, Tout le monde y dan-se, dan-se

Sur le pont d'A - vig - non, Tout le monde y danse en rond.

English Version

On the Bridge of Avignon

On the bridge of Avignon,
Everyone is dancing, dancing
On the bridge of Avignon,
Everyone is dancing round.

The handsome boys go like this
The pretty girls go like that

On the bridge of Avignon,
Everyone is dancing, dancing
On the bridge of Avignon,
Everyone is dancing round.

TSD 02267-8 • *Multicultural Music*

FRENCH RECIPES

Crêpe Suzette

Ingredients:

4 large eggs, 1 1/4 cups flour, sifted, 1 tsp. salt, 3 Tbsp. sugar, 1 3/4 cups milk, 2 Tbsp. butter, 1 tsp. orange extract

1. Beat eggs.
2. Slowly add flour and salt.
3. In a pan, heat the milk with the butter and sugar until butter is completely melted (do not boil).
4. Gradually blend the milk mixture with the egg batter until smooth.
5. Add orange extract.
6. Chill batter for 1–2 hours or overnight before using.
7. Heat a nonstick pan until hot.
8. Pour enough batter to just cover the bottom of the pan by swirling the pan.
9. When the edges are dry, flip the crêpe over.
10. Cook for 1 minute.
11. Remove crêpe; fold in quarters. Set aside on plate.
12. Dip the folded crêpe in warm orange sauce before serving.
    Variation: Dip in warm chocolate syrup. Try different sauces or various jellies (grape, strawberry, raspberry). Offer the children spoonfuls of choices.

Orange Sauce for Crêpe Suzette

Ingredients:

6 oz. frozen orange juice mixed with 6 oz. water, 1 Tbsp. of lemon juice, 4 Tbsp. sugar, 3 Tbsp. unsalted butter, 1 tsp. rum extract (optional)

1. Mix all ingredients
2. Heat (on low setting) until consistency of light syrup.

French Toast

Ingredients:

6 eggs, 1 cup milk, 1/2 tsp. salt, 1 Tbsp. sugar, oil, 8 slices thick bread (preferably 3 days old), butter, maple syrup, jelly or powdered sugar

1. Slightly beat eggs, milk, salt, and sugar.
2. Heat oil in pan.
3. Dip bread in batter and cook each side on medium heat until golden brown.
4. Serve hot with butter and syrup, jelly, or sugar.

Croque Monsieur

Ingredients:

4 slices Swiss cheese, 4 slices cooked ham, 8 slices bread, 2 eggs, 1/4 cup milk, 2 Tbsp. butter

1. Make 4 ham and cheese sandwiches. Trim away any excess ham or cheese.
2. Beat eggs and milk together.
3. Melt butter over low heat.
4. Dip sandwiches in batter and cook each side until golden brown.
5. Cut in quarters and serve to children.

Quiche Lorraine
an open-faced egg tart
Ingredients:
1 frozen pie crust, 1 tsp. butter, 4 eggs (lightly beaten), 1 cup heavy cream, 1/2 tsp. salt, pinch of pepper, 1/2 cup cheddar cheese (shredded)
Add your choice of the following ingredients:
6 slices of fried bacon, 1/2 cup of diced ham, sliced mushrooms, diced onions, diced green or red pepper
1. Follow directions on package to prepare the pie crust.
2. Add the ingredients to the pie crust.
3. Bake at 375° until knife inserted in center of pie comes out clean – approximately 30 minutes.

Profiteroles aux Chocolats (Chocolate Topped Cream Puffs)
Ingredients:
1/2 cup water, 4 Tbsp. unsalted butter, 1/4 tsp. vanilla extract, 2 Tbsp. sugar, 1/2 cup sifted all-purpose flour, 2 large eggs, vanilla pudding, chocolate syrup
1. Bring first four ingredients to a boil over medium heat. Stir occasionally with wooden spoon. Remove from heat.
2. Stir flour into the liquid. Return to stove cooking and stirring until the mixture forms a mass, leaving the sides of the pan. Remove from heat.
3. Add 1 egg at a time, beating it into the pastry.
4. Test the pastry. Upon lifting your spoon, the pastry should hang down 2 to 3 inches. If it does not, add a little more egg. If it runs too much, add a little more flour.
5. Cool slightly.
6. Drop batter by heaping tablespoons 3 inches apart onto a greased baking sheet or form small mounds using a pastry bag.
7. Brush the cream puffs very slightly with a beaten egg.
8. Bake at 400° for 25 minutes until firm to the touch. Remove from the oven and place on rack.
9. While warm, make a slit on the sides of each cream puff with a sharp knife.
10. Cool the puffs.
11. Fill with cooked vanilla pudding and drizzle with chocolate syrup.

Tarte Tatin (Upside-Down Caramelized Apple Tart)
Ingredients:
4 lbs. crisp apples, 5 oz. sugar, 1 tsp. cinnamon, 3 oz. melted butter, pastry sticks or any sweet pastry crust, powdered sugar, 3/4 pt. heavy cream
1. Peel and core apples. Cut in lengthwise slices, approximately 1/8" thick.
2. Mix with cinnamon and 2 oz. sugar.
3. Sprinkle half the remaining sugar in a heavily buttered 9" baking dish.
4. Place 1/3 of the apples in the dish, then top with 1/3 of the melted butter. Repeat in the same order.

Activities

1. Make a matching game for the days of the week. Copy, cut apart, and glue the French words for the days of the week onto individual 3" by 5" cards (patterns found on page 60). Print the English words for the days of the week onto individual 3" by 5" cards. Mix the cards and instruct the students to match the English to the French.

2. For the Tour de France, students can make individual racers. Make copies of the French racer (found on page 60) on white cardstock. Students can elect to add red polka-dots to the racer's white shirt or color it yellow or green as the lyrics explain in the song *Watching the Race*. Sing this song as well as the song *Tour de France*. (Both songs found on page 51.)

3. Two French brothers were the first Europeans to successfully launch a balloon to carry human beings. Make a bulletin board display with nine hot air balloons. Place the numerals one through nine in a circle in the center of each of the balloons. Read them in French.

4. Make a puppet theatre. (Patterns are found on pages 61-64.) Make the three puppets, Guignol, Madame de Bois and Monsieur Béné. The puppet instructions are for a puppet with a papier mâché head. The following directions are for a puppet with a felt head: for each puppet, cut and sew two pieces of felt in the shape of the body with the neck and head attached. Cut two round pieces of felt in the size of the head. Stuff batting material in between the two circles of felt before sewing them closed. With a glue gun, attach the padded circle onto the head part of the puppet. Color and glue copies of the faces onto the padded circles.

5. Encourage the students to use the three puppets to sing the song *The Three Marionettes* found on page 49 and the song, *Les Petites Marionnettes,* found on page 53.

6. Use the backdrop building scenery from pages 63-64 as a visual aid for the song *Bon Appetit* (page 50). Discuss with the students the four types of stores as defined in the word list.

7. Make game cards with French numerals.
    a. Use the numeral cards as flash cards so that students can learn to read the French numerals.
    b. Use two sets of cards to play a memory match game.
    c. Use one set of French numerals and one set of English numerals. Students can match the French numerals with the correct English numerals.

8. One holiday that French children enjoy is The Feast of the Three Kings on January 6th. Children gather to "draw out the king," *tirer le roi*. A large, round puff pastry is baked with a single bean or tiny plastic figurine inside of it. It is called **la galette des rois** (la ga-let day rwa). One whole almond is substituted for the bean in this version. The child who finds the almond becomes the king or queen, is given a gold and silver paper crown and leads the march around the room.

PROJECT
The following treat is an adaptation of a delicious French recipe.

La Galette des Rois (Cake of the Kings)
light, flaky pastry dessert
1. Buy frozen pastry shells.
2. Brush each shell with egg yolk and water mixture (1 beaten egg yolk with 1 Tbsp water).
3. Sprinkle lightly with sugar.
4. Bake according to package directions.
5. Cook on wire rack.
6. Make instant vanilla pudding adding 1 Tbsp. almond extract to the liquid
7. Remove top of pastry shell.
8. Place one whole almond into only one puff shell.
9. Spoon pudding into each shell
10. The child who finds the almond in his or her pastry, becomes the king or queen, is crowned, and leads the march around the room.

9. The French are known for their great cooking and their appreciation of well-prepared food. Ask parents to assist the students with making and serving French foods one morning. Have French toast, Quiche Lorraine, and Croque Monsieur. Students should be involved in the preparation, serving, and cleanup.

10. Ask parents for a volunteer to make crêpe suzette for snacks. The crêpes can be made at home and heated in a microwave at school. The orange sauce can be kept warm in an electric pot. The children will also enjoy selecting different sauces or jellies for their crêpes.

11. Obtain a recording of *Carmen* for the children to hear. Play the *Habanera* and the *Toreador Song*. Read a synopsis of the story and tell it to the students.

12. For more information write or call: French Cultural Service, Information Service, 972 Fifth Avenue, New York, NY 10021, Telephone (212) 439-1400 or Embassy of France, 4101 Reservoir Road, NW, Washington, DC 20007, Telephone (202) 994-6000.

BOOKS TO READ

MADELEINE SERIES
by Ludwig Bemelmans
Madeleine
Madeleine's Rescue
Madeleine's Christmas
Madeleine and the Gypsies
Madeleine and the Bad Hat
A series of easy-reader books about a young French girl living in an orphanage in France

BABAR SERIES
by Jean de Brunhoff
The Story of Babar the Little Elephant
The Travels of Babar
Babar and Father Christmas
Babar and the King
by Laurent de Brunhoff
Babar and His Children
Babar Loses His Crown
Meet Babar and His Family
Babar's French Lesson
A series of easy-reader books about an elephant who runs away from the jungle, goes to live with an old lady in Paris and quickly adapts to French ways; he later returns to the jungle and becomes king

Mirette on the High Wire
Emily Arnold
Mirette learns tightrope-walking from Monsieur Bellini, not knowing that he is a celebrated artist who no longer performs because of fear

The Inside-Outside Book of Paris
Roxit Munro
Artistic, colorful illustrations and simple text portray Paris highlights

A Brother for the Orphelines
Natalie Carlson
A story about a baby boy being left at an all-girl orphanage in France

A Family under the Bridge
Natalie Carlson
Humorous story of Armand, an old Parisian homeless man, who finds a ready family under a Paris bridge

Viviane Lives in France
Day Hampton
An easy-reader with black and white photographs of a young French girl

FRENCH RACER

1. Cut out wheels and racer.
2. Attach wheels to bicycle frame with brad fasteners, as shown.

DAYS OF THE WEEK

	mardi
samedi	**mercredi**
dimanche	**jeudi**
lundi	**vendredi**

Guignol Puppet Instructions

You will need:

newspaper
masking tape
cardboard tube
diluted white glue or wheat paste
white paint

selection of poster paints
nontoxic clear gloss varnish
fabric, felt
needle and thread

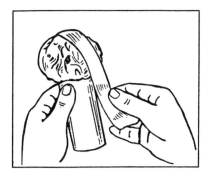  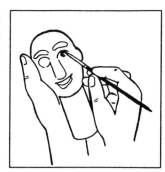

1. Beginning with puppet's head, crumple a newspaper page into a ball, and tape it onto the cardboard tube with masking tape. Use extra masking tape to help shape the head.

2. Tear newspaper into strips and soak in diluted glue or paste. Cover the puppet's head with four layers of papier mâché.

3. Form the puppet's features by squashing glue-soaked strips of newspaper into small pellets of pulp and sticking them into place. Cover over the pulp with two layers of short, thin newspaper strips.

4. Allow the head to dry overnight in a warm place. Lightly smooth it with sandpaper and then prime it with two coats of white acrylic paint. When it is dry, draw features on the puppet and decorate the head with poster paints, adding detail with black permanent marker. Let the head dry overnight and seal it with two coats of clear gloss varnish.

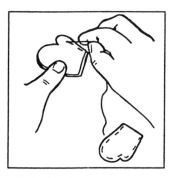 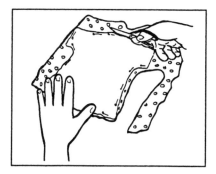 

5. Cut the hands out of felt, using pattern provided. Make the hands by stitching the two layers of felt together with thread.

6. Cut out costume using pattern provided, double-layered. Turn inside out and sew around, leaving an opening for the head, hands, and the bottom of the costume.

7. Stitch hands to the cuffs of the costume. Glue costume to neck of puppet's head securely with glue.

PUPPET PATTERNS

Guignol   **Madame de Bois**   **Monsieur Béné**

Japan

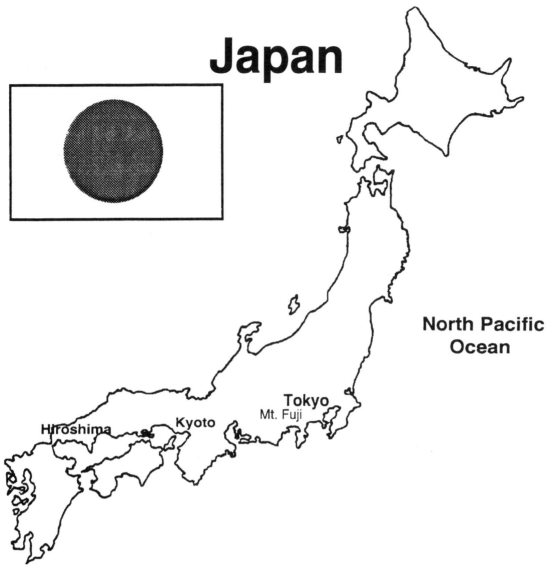

North Pacific Ocean

Tokyo
Mt. Fuji
Kyoto
Hiroshima

Japan is a country in the Pacific Ocean made up of four large islands and many smaller ones. The Japanese call their country Nippon or Nihon which means source of the sun. Their flag is a red sun on a white field. Among Japan's major cities, two that can be found on Honshu, the biggest island, are Tokyo and Kyoto. Kyoto became the capital of Japan in 794. With its beautiful temples and historic traditions, it has become a most popular mecca for tourists. Tokyo is the nation's present-day capital. Japan is an important agricultural and industrial center. Japan, the Land of the Rising Sun, is covered with mountains and hills. Fujiyama or Mount Fuji is Japan's highest peak. Japanese-style meals are usually eaten with chopsticks. Rice is the basic food of many Japanese. They also eat a lot of fish. The traditional Japanese clothing is the kimono. This long, loose robe of cotton or silk is tied around the waist with a sash called an obi. Most women and girls wear dressy kimonos only on special occasions because they are very expensive. For relaxing at home, the Japanese may wear a simple, lightweight kimono. But outside the home, most prefer western-style clothing. The Japanese wear *geta*, wooden sandals with two strips of wood across the soles, or *zori*, flat sandals with rubber soles, when wearing Japanese-style clothing. Slippers are the only footwear worn at home. Two types of wrestling, judo and sumo, are very popular sports.

Word List

Numerals

ichi (ee-chee):	one
ni (nee):	two
san (san):	three
shi (shee):	four
go (go):	five
roku (ro-koo):	six
nana (na-na):	seven
hachi (ha-chee):	eight
kyu (kee-yoo):	nine
ju (joo):	ten

Pronunciation Key

ay:	as in t**ray**; **a**lien
y:	as in b**y**; **lie**; s**igh**
ee:	as in l**ea**p; pr**ie**st
u:	as in d**u**st; p**u**n
a:	as in l**a**h dee d**a**h
e:	as in s**e**ven; r**e**st
i:	as in p**i**n; b**ee**r; m**i**rror
o:	as in p**o**ke; l**oa**n; r**oa**m
oo:	as in l**oo**ny; s**ou**p
j:	as in **j**am; **g**iraffe
g:	as in **g**ate; a**g**ain
s:	as in **S**anta; help**s**
z:	as in **z**oo; ea**s**y

Parts of the Body

ago (a-go):	chin
atama (a-ta-ma):	head
hana (ha-na):	nose
hoho (ho-ho):	cheek
kami (ka-mee):	hair
kao (ka-o):	face
kata (ka-ta):	shoulder
kubi (koo-bee):	neck
kuchibiru (koo-chee-bir-oo):	lip
mimi (mee-mee):	ear
onaka (o-na-ka):	stomach
senaka (sen-a-ka):	back
yubi (yoo-bee):	fingers

Colors

aka (a-ka):	red
ao (a-o):	blue
kiiro (kee-ee-ro):	yellow
midori (mee-do-ree):	green
murasaki (moor-a-sa-kee):	purple
orenji (o-ren-jee):	orange

Translations:
anone (a-no-nee): let me tell you something
A so desu ne (a so des-ne): I agree
Banzai (ban-zy): just like "three cheers," Banzai! Banzai! Banzai! and raised arms denote celebration
Fuku wa uchi (foo-koo wa oo-chee): good luck, enter
Ii tenki (ee-ee ten-kee): it's a nice day
Ki o tsukete ne (kee ot-soo-ke-te ne): Be careful, dear
Konnichiwa (ko-nee-chee-wa): hello
Matsuri (mat-sir-ee): festival time
Mo ichido (mo ee-chee-do): again, please
moshi moshi (mo-shee mo-shee): I say (used as the beginning of a telephone conversation)
Naoko (ny-yo-ko): Japanese girl's name
Oni wa soto (o-nee wa so-to): Oni, go out
Oshi mai (a-shee ma-ee): That's the end
Sadako (sa-da-ko): Japanese girl's name
Sayonara (sy-o-na-ra): good-bye
Setsubun (set-soo-boon): Bean Throwing Day

Definitions
carp streamers: streamers in the shape of carp, cut from cloth. Used to celebrate hope for sons as healthy and strong as the carp that swim against the stream. Flown on and around Kodomo-no-Hi (May 5th)
chopsticks: two sticks made from wood, ivory, or plastic, used as eating utensils by many Asian cultures
crane: wading bird with long legs, neck, and bill
Kodomo-no-hi (ko-do-mo no hee): May 5th, Children's Day
Kyoto (kee-o-to): large historic city; was capital of Japan from 794–1868
Mount Fuji (foo-jee): Mount Fuji—also called Fujiyama. Highest mountain in Japan, considered sacred; has become a symbol for all of Japan
Oni (o-nee): mischievous fictional creature that has long teeth, many horns, bulging eyes, and is orange, purple and green
origami: art of folding paper into decorative objects
peace cranes: origami cranes symbolizing peace and hope
Peace Memorial Park: Hiroshima memorial park in honor memory of the victims of the atom bomb that was dropped by the United States in 1945 during World War II
Tokyo (to-kee-yo): capital of Japan

This song is an invitation from a Japanese child to come and visit Japan. Japanese family life is very child-centered. On March 3rd, a Doll Festival is held to wish happiness to girls. Imperial court dolls are displayed. On May 5th, military dolls are displayed with the hope that boys will grow up to possess the Japanese ideals of manhood. This day, once called Boy's Festival, is now called Children's Day, Kodomo-no-Hi. It is celebrated for boys and girls. Carp streamers are flown to express hopes that the children will be as vigorously healthy as the carp that swim against the stream.

COME WITH ME
(Melody: This Old Man)

Come with me, you will see
I'm so proud of my country
I was born in Japan so
very far away
I will take you there today!

Come with me, you will see
I'm so proud of my country
There are so many mountains
very, very tall
Mount Fuji is highest of all!

Come with me, you will see
I'm so proud of my country
We will go to Kyoto and
see the ancient shrines
Eat fancy cakes and taste rice wine.

Come with me, you will see
I'm so proud of my country
We will fly carp streamers on
Kodomo-no-Hi
Children's Day is fun you see!

Word List: *Mount Fuji, Kyoto, carp streamers, Kodomo-no-Hi*

Learning the colors in Japanese is fun when sung to this familiar melody.

COLORS
(Melody: Down By The Station)

Yellow is kiiro
Purple's murasaki
I learned all the colors
From my friends in Japan
Orange is orenji
They call green "midori"
Red is aka; blue, ao.

Word List: *kiiro, murasaki, orenji, midori, aka, ao*

The traditional way to begin a telephone conversation in Japan is "moshi moshi."

The following song can be sung by two individuals, two groups, or two puppets.

TELEPHONE TALK
(Melody: London Bridges)

Child 1:
Moshi moshi, anone
Anone, anone
Moshi moshi, anone
Ii tenki

Child 2:
Moshi moshi, anone
Anone, anone
Moshi moshi, anone
A so desu ne

Word List: *moshi moshi, anone, Ii tenki, A so desu ne*

Sing the following song in an echo fashion to teach the numerals.

JAPANESE NUMERALS
(Melody: Are You Sleeping?)

Ichi, ni, san
Ichi, ni, san
Shi, go, roku
Shi, go, roku
Nana, hachi, kyu, ju
Nana, hachi, kyu, ju
Mo ichido; Mo ichido.

Ichi, ni, san
Ichi, ni, san
Shi, go, roku
Shi, go, roku
Nana, hachi, kyu, ju
Nana, hachi, kyu, ju
Oshi mai; Oshi mai.

Word List: *ichi, ni, san, shi, go, roku, nana, hachi, kyu, ju, Mo ichido, Oshi mai*

The bow is the basic form of greeting in Japan. While standing, bring your legs together, bend your body forward from the waist, and lower your head. Bow each time you sing "Konnichiwa" and "Sayonara" in this song of greeting and farewell.

I VISIT NAOKO
(Melody: Oh, Susanna)

Oh, I'd like to visit my dear friend
Naoko is her name
I must take a plane to Tokyo
So very far away.

Sayonara, I said to mom and dad
I must say good-bye and leave you now
But I'll be back again.

Sayonara, they smiled at me and said,
It's so nice of you to visit her
Ki o tsukete ne

Well, Naoko smiled at me and bowed,
My friend please do come in
I took off my shoes and stepped inside
She looked at me and grinned.

Hello, hello! Konnichiwa, my friend!
It's so nice to see you looking well
She smiled and bowed again.

Hello, hello! Konnichiwa, my friend!
I'm so glad that I could come today
And see you once again.

Well, Naoko brought me fish to eat
With chopsticks made of wood
I dropped the fish right on my lap
I did the best I could.

Hello, hello! Konnichiwa, my friend!
It's so nice to see you looking well
She smiled and bowed again.

Hello, hello! Konnichiwa, my friend!
I'm so glad that I could come today
And see you once again.

Well, Naoko asked me to sit down
And fold some birds and planes,
Origami is her favorite art
We fold one hundred cranes.

Hello, hello! Konnichiwa, my friend!
It's so nice to see you looking well
She smiled and bowed again.

Hello, hello! Konnichiwa, my friend!
I'm so glad that I could come today
And see you once again.

Well, Naoko brought me tea and cake
'Twas nearly time to go
With a tear she looked at me and said,
My friend I'll miss you so.

Sayonara, I said to my dear friend,
I must say good-bye and leave you now
But I'll be back again!

Sayonara, Naoko smiled and said,
It was nice of you to visit me
Ki o tsukete ne.

Word List: *Naoko, Tokyo, sayonara, Ki o tsukete ne, konnichiwa, chopsticks, origami*

BODY PARTS
(Melody: Love Somebody—Yes I Do)

Tap your head, and say "atama"
Tap your nose, and call it "hana"
Tap your shoulder; call it "kata"
Shake your fingers now and say "yubi."
    Touch your neck and call it "kubi"
    Touch your ear, and call it "mimi"
    Touch your hair, and call it "kami"
    Shake your fingers now and say "yubi."
Wash your face and call it "kao"
Wash your cheek and call it "hoho"
Wash your chin and call it "ago"
Shake your fingers now and say "yubi."

Word List: *atama, hana, kata, yubi, kami, mimi, kubi, kao, hoho, ago*

Invite the children to copy the leader as they tap and name the parts of the body in English and Japanese.

The leader will tap each body part the number of times equal to the number of syllables in its Japanese word. The children will copy the leader and conclude by cheering Banzai!

BANZAI
(Melody: Bluebird)

Leader: *tap ear, nose, and lip*
Mimi, hana, kuchibiru
Mimi, hana, kuchibiru
Mimi, hana, kuchibiru
Now show me you can do it!

Children: *tap ear, nose and lip*
Mimi, hana, kuchibiru
Mimi, hana, kuchibiru
Mimi, hana, kuchibiru
Banzai 'cause I can do it—Banzai!

Leader: *tap chin, neck, and stomach*
Ago, kubi, onaka
Ago, kubi, onaka
Ago, kubi, onaka
Now show me you can do it!

Children: *tap chin, neck, and stomach*
Ago, kubi, onaka
Ago, kubi, onaka
Ago, kubi, onaka
Banzai 'cause I can do it—Banzai!

Leader: *tap hair, shoulder, and back*
Kami, kata, senaka
Kami, kata, senaka
Kami, kata, senaka
Now show me you can do it!

Children: *tap hair, shoulder, and back*
Kami, kata, senaka
Kami, kata, senaka
Kami, kata, senaka
Banzai 'cause I can do it—Banzai!

> **Word List:** *Banzai, mimi, hana, kuchibiru, ago, kubi, onaka, kami, kata, senaka*

Matsuri means festival time in Japan. The Japanese are able to keep their traditions alive because of their various celebrations which take place all year long.

MATSURI
(Melody: Sakura, page 74)

Go to sleep; go to sleep
Close your eyes and dream lovely dreams
Matsuri is festival time
In the morning, we'll celebrate
Setsubun* is here when you wake
We will go; we will go
We will celebrate soon!

> **Word List:** *Matsuri, Setsubun*

One fun festival is Bean Throwing Day known as Setsubun. It is the oldest matsuri and is celebrated on February 2nd. One throws beans out the door and windows while chanting "Oni wa soto" (Oni go out). Then beans are thrown inside the home while chanting "Fuku wa uchi" (good luck come inside).

Legends state that the crane is a bird that can live as long as a thousand years. This is why the crane is a symbol for long life in Japan. It has become a symbol of peace throughout the world because of the story of Sadako Sasaki who died at the age of twelve. Sadako was a victim of radiation disease caused by the atom bomb that was dropped on Hiroshima in 1945. She believed that if she could fold a thousand paper cranes, she would recover. She was unable to complete the task but her story has inspired millions of children all over the world to send paper cranes to Hiroshima to express their hopes for peace. At Peace Park in Hiroshima, you can find a statue of Sadako holding a golden crane in outstretched hands. Engraved on the base of the statue are these words: "This is our cry. This is our prayer; peace in the world."

PEACE CRANES
(Melody: Billy Boy)

Is it true that the cranes live so long, live so long?
Is it true that they live to one thousand?
Can you fold just four more cranes?
You can make them all the same
Tell the world that we need to have one thousand!

Is it true that the cranes bring good luck, bring good luck?
Is it true that they live to one thousand?
Can you fold just three more cranes?
You can make them all the same
Tell the world that we need to have one thousand!

Is it true that the cranes fly so far, fly so far?
Is it true that they live to one thousand?
Can you fold just two more cranes?
You can make them both the same
Tell the world that we need to have one thousand!

Is it true that the cranes will bring peace, will bring peace?
Is it true that they live to one thousand?
Can you fold just one more crane?
You can make it look the same
Tell the world that we need to have one thousand!

> **Word List:** cranes, Peace Crane

PEACE IN THE WORLD
(Melody: Down In The Valley)

This is our cry now
This is our prayer
Peace in the world, friends
Peace everywhere!

Little Sadako
No longer here
Hurt by the anger
Hurt by the fear.

This is our cry now
This is our prayer
Peace in the world, friends
Peace everywhere!

Come to the Peace Park
Come bring your cranes
No longer strangers
Friends once again.

This is our cry now
This is our prayer
Peace in the world, friends
Peace everywhere!

> **Word List:** Sadako, Peace Park

AIZU LULLABY
(Aizu Komori Uta)

The Aizu District of Japan is known for its beautiful mountains and lakes. It is from this region that this lullaby comes. This same melody is sung throughout the nation and is often used in popular songs.

Slowly and soothingly

Hi ya!— Go to— sleep,— ba-by,— Hi ya!— Go to— sleep.————
Ho ra— nei ro— ne— nei ro,— Ho ra— nei ro— ya.——

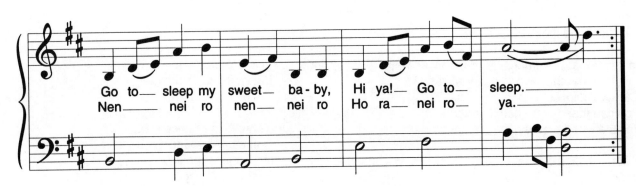

Go to— sleep my sweet ba-by, Hi ya!— Go to— sleep.————
Nen— nei ro nen— nei ro Ho ra— nei ro— ya.

2. Nurse has gone to visit her family,
    She will bring them joy.
    When she returns to you, my baby,
    She will bring you a toy.

   TSD 02267-8 • *Multicultural Music*

KAGOME, KAGOME
(Bird in Cage)

Moderately, strongly accented

Ka - go - me, ka - go - me, Ka - go no na - ka no

to - ri wa, I - tsu I - tsu de - ya - ru?

Yo - a - ke no ba - n ni, Tsu - ru to Ka - me to

su - bet - ta, U - shi - ro no sho - men da - a - re?

English translation:

The bird in the cage,   On a dark night,
The bird in the cage,   Toward the dawn,
When will the bird   The crane and the turtle misstepped
Get out of the cage?   Who is right behind you?

       TSD 02267-8 • *Multicultural Music*

SAKURA
(Cherry Trees)

Sa - ku - ra! Sa - ku - ra! Ya - ya - i no so - ra
Cher - ry trees, cher - ry trees, Bloom so bright in A - pril

wa, Mi - wa - ta - su ka - ghi - ri; Ka - su - mi ka?
breeze. Like a mist or float - ing cloud; Fra - grance fills the

Ku - mo - ka? Ni - o - i zo i - zu - ru;
air a - round, Shad - ows flit a - long the ground.

I - za ya! I - za ya! Mi - ni yu - ka - n.
Come, oh, come! Come, oh, come! Come, see cher - ry trees!

TSD 02267-8 • *Multicultural Music*

Dashi
Ingredients:
1/2 cup dried bonito flakes, 2 cups water
1. Bring water to a boil. Add bonito flakes.
2. Bring to a boil again, then remove from heat.
3. After bonito flakes sink to the bottom, strain through a cloth. Discard the flakes.

Dashi From Kombu
Ingredients:
2 cups water, 4" long kombu, 1/2 cup dried bonito flakes
1. Wipe kombu lightly with a dry cloth. Do not wipe off the white powdery surface, since that provides the unique savory flavor.
2. Soak kombu in water for 30 minutes, then heat. Before water comes to a boil (as it starts to bubble), remove kombu. Do not overcook, because flavor becomes too strong.
3. Add dried bonito flakes. When water comes to a boil, remove from heat and leave until bonito flakes sink to the bottom.
4. Strain through a cloth and discard used flakes.

Japanese Rice
Ingredients:
2 1/2 cups short grain rice, 3 cups water
1. Put rice in a pot. Add water to rinse and stir. Drain. Repeat 3–4 times, or until water runs almost clear.
2. Add the 3 cups of water and allow to soak for 30–60 minutes.
3. Cook on medium to low heat for 10 minutes, gradually bringing to a vigorous boil. Reduce heat to prevent bubbling over and continue cooking for 5 minutes.
4. Reduce heat again and simmer for 15 minutes.
5. Turn heat to high for 5 seconds to evaporate any excess water.
6. Cover and let steam for 10 minutes.
7. Remove lid quickly to prevent excess water from dripping onto rice. Use a wet wooden spatula/spoon to lightly mix rice in a folding motion from the bottom up so that rice is fluffy.
8. Dish into individual bowls. (If core of rice remains hard, moisten with sake [1 Tbsp. per 2 1/2 cups of rice] and simmer on low heat for 7 -8 minutes.)

Niku-Jaga (Flavored Beef and Potatoes)
Ingredients:
4 medium potatoes, 7 oz. beef or pork, sliced thinly, 1 Tbsp. ginger, finely chopped, 2 Tbsp. sugar, 2 Tbsp. sake, 3 Tbsp. soy sauce
1. Peel and cut potatoes into large pieces. Let potatoes soak in cold water for 5 minutes.
2. Cut meat into 2" pieces.
3. Mix rest of ingredients in a saucepan. Bring to a boil.
4. Add the meat and again bring to a boil.
5. Add potatoes and enough water to cover all the ingredients. Place a plate or some kind of a lid directly on top of the ingredients.
6. Bring to a boil. Reduce heat and simmer until potatoes are cooked.

Okonomi-Yaki (Northern Style)
Ingredients:
2 cups flour, 1 tsp. baking powder, dash of salt, 1 cup dashi (see page 75), 1 large cabbage, 4 oz. ground pork, vegetable oil, dried bonito flakes
1. Sift dry ingredients into large bowl.
2. Slowly add dashi until smooth, but do not over-mix.
3. Cover bowl with plastic wrap and allow to set for 30 minutes.
4. Cut cabbage leaves into thin strips, omitting the hard part.
5. Add cabbage, egg, and pork to batter and gently mix.
6. Pour out batter in pancake form onto a greased heated skillet and cook until bubbles form. Flip.
7. Brush with sauce.
8. Before removing from skillet, sprinkle with dried bonito flakes.

Oyako-Donburi
Ingredients:
cooked rice for 4 bowls, 4 oz. chicken, 2 large onions, 4 eggs (slightly beaten), 12 Tbsp. dashi (page 75), 4 tsp. sugar, 2 Tbsp. mirin, 4 Tbsp. soy sauce
1. Slice onion and chicken.
2. Mix sugar, mirin, soy sauce, and dashi in a saucepan and bring to a boil.
3. Add chicken and cook. Add onion and cook until translucent, then add eggs and cook. Remove from heat after 2 minutes.
4. Spoon on top of bowls of cooked rice and serve.

Teriyaki Chicken
Ingredients:
1/4 cup soy sauce, 8 oz. chicken breast (boned and cut in pieces), oil, 1 cup mushrooms, 1 cup onions (chopped), 1/4 cup soy sauce, 1 cup bean sprouts, oil
1. Marinate chicken in soy sauce for 8 hours.
2. Saute chicken in oil for 5 minutes or until brown.
3. Add mushrooms, onions and soy sauce. Heat well.
4. Add bean sprouts and serve with rice.

Fried Rice
Ingredients:
2 Tbsp. onion, minced, 1/3 cup oil, leftover meat or chicken scraps, 2 eggs, 1 cup bean sprouts, 4 cups cooked rice, 1/2 tsp. salt
1. Cook onion in oil until translucent. Add meat.
2. Scramble eggs in another pan.
3. Add eggs and other ingredients to the meat and onions. Heat through and serve.

Activity Ideas

1. Make carp streamers. Copy the pattern on page 82. Children can color and cut out the carp and they can then paste it onto either a paper lunch bag with the bottom cut off or onto the end of a 12" x 12" sheet of paper. Roll and tape the paper into a cylinder so that the wind can blow through it. Adhere gummed reinforcement circles by the mouth of the fish (inside and outside) and on the opposite side (inside and outside); tie string to both sides. Hang outdoors in the wind.

2. Children will enjoy origami, the Japanese art of folding paper. Follow the illustrations on pages 79-81. Many origami books can be found in libraries with projects that range from the simple to the complex. Origami paper can be bought in different sizes and colors at art and craft stores and some toy shops. You can also cut durable paper into squares; popular sizes are 3, 5 1/2, and 7 inches. Invite children to begin with the cup on pape 79. It is the simplest to do and can actually hold a small amount of water.

3. Celebrate World Peace Day on a day of your choice during the school year! (The actual date is August 6th.) It is a memorial day set aside throughout the world to recall those who have died from the dropping of the atomic bomb. Read *Sadako and the Thousand Paper Cranes* by Eleanor Coerr and tell the story to the students. Invite the children to fold paper cranes which can be hung around the room. Sing the songs *Peace Cranes* and *Peace In The World*. Peace cranes can be sent to Peace Park in Hiroshima to be placed at the memorial statue. For current requirements write to: The Hiroshima Peace Memorial Center 1–3 Nakajimacho, Nakaku Hiroshima, Japan 730.

4. Have the children create stick puppets of a Japanese boy and girl. Use the puppets with the song *I Visit Naoko*. Invite the children to use the puppets to act out a story of a Japanese boy and girl who have been going to school and learning English. The puppets can talk to each other using both English and Japanese words and sayings. The puppets can also sing *Telephone Talk*.

5. Arrange with a local Japanese restaurant to donate chopsticks (hashi) for each of the students. Order or make teriyaki or fried rice. Demonstrate how to use the chopsticks and invite the children to use them as they eat the Japanese food.

6. Have the children set up the classroom as a restaurant offering Japanese food. Offer parents the Japanese recipes provided in this book and ask them to cook the food for this dramatization. Children can design menus and list foods available. Some can be waiters and waitresses who take orders and serve food and others can dish out the orders. Children can write sayings on slips of paper for fortune cookies, decorate the room with carp streamers or paper cranes, and borrow Japanese recordings from the library for background music.

7. Set up a sushi bar. Buy sticky rice from a Japanese store. Cook according to directions and cool. Have children roll into balls, placing the item of their choice in the center of their rice ball. Some suggestions are peas, cut up carrots, and tuna.

8. Obtain more information on Japan by writing or calling: Japan Information Center, Consulate General of Japan, 299 Park Avenue, 16th Floor, New York, NY 10171-0025, Telephone: (212) 371-8222 or Embassy of Japan, 2520 Massachusetts Avenue, NW, Washington, DC 20008, Telephone: (202) 387-6101.

BOOKS TO READ

A to Zen
Ruth Wells
A book of Japanese culture

The Boy Who Drew Cats
Arthur Levine
A Japanese legend of a boy's passion for art

The Crane Girl
Veronika M. Charles
After the birth of a sibling, Yoshiko decides to go and live among the cranes

Crow Boy
Taro Yashima
A story about a young Japanese boy who can imitate the sound of crows

The Eyes of a Cat
Demi
Japanese poems

Festival in My Heart
Bruno Peter Navasky
Poems written by Japanese elementary school students

The Funny Little Woman
Arlene Mosel
While chasing a dumpling, a little lady is captured by the oni

The Inch High Samurai
Shiro Kasamatsuln
A story of a little boy no bigger than your thumb

Journey through Japan
Richard Tames
A book for elementary school children about the people, culture, geography and history of Japan

**The Magic Listening Cap—
More Folk Tales from Japan**
Yoshiko Uchida
Among these folk stories is the well-known, tale "The Rice Cake That Rolled Away"

Mieko and the Fifth Treasure
Eleanor Coerr
Ten-year-old Mieko goes to Nagasaki to stay with her grandparents after the dropping of the atomic bomb

Mighty Mountain and the Three Strong Women
Irene Hedlund
A Japanese folk tale about a young sumo wrestler

The Paper Crane
Molly Bang
The gift of a magical paper crane changes a man's fortunes

Sadako
Eleanor Coerr
A Japanese girl's story becomes the world's hope for peace

The Snow Wife
Robert San Soreci
A Japanese woodcutter encounters the Snow Woman

Thanksgiving at Obachans
by Janet Mitsui Brown
Thanksgiving at a Japanese grandmother's house

Cup

1

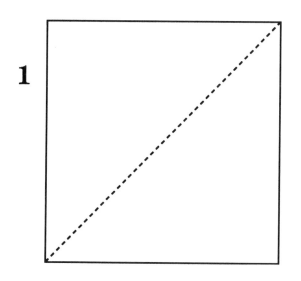

2

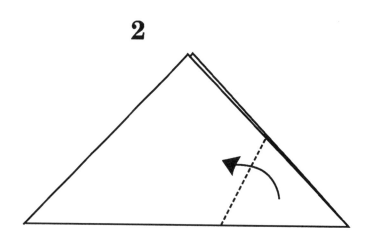

3

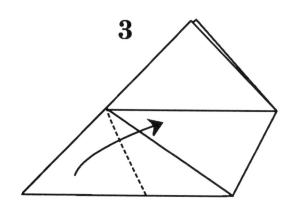

4

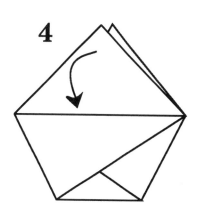

5

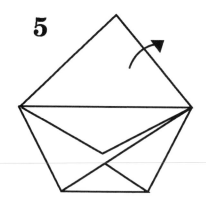

6

Tuck in outer flap

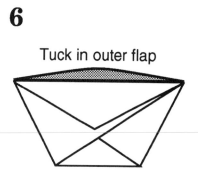

TSD 02267-8 • *Multicultural Music*

Hat

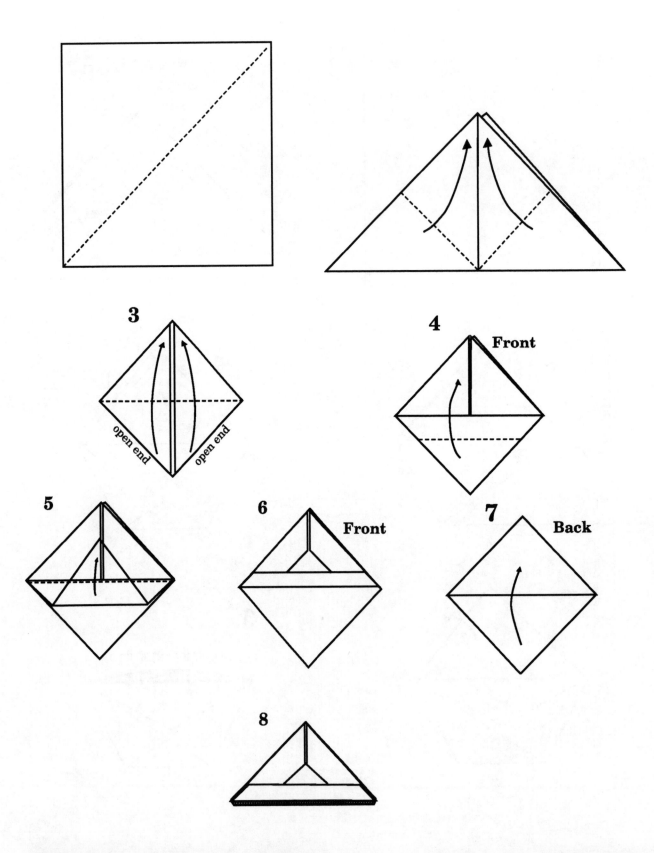

3

open end   open end

4   **Front**

5

6   **Front**

7   **Back**

8

          TSD 02267-8 • *Multicultural Music*

Peace Crane

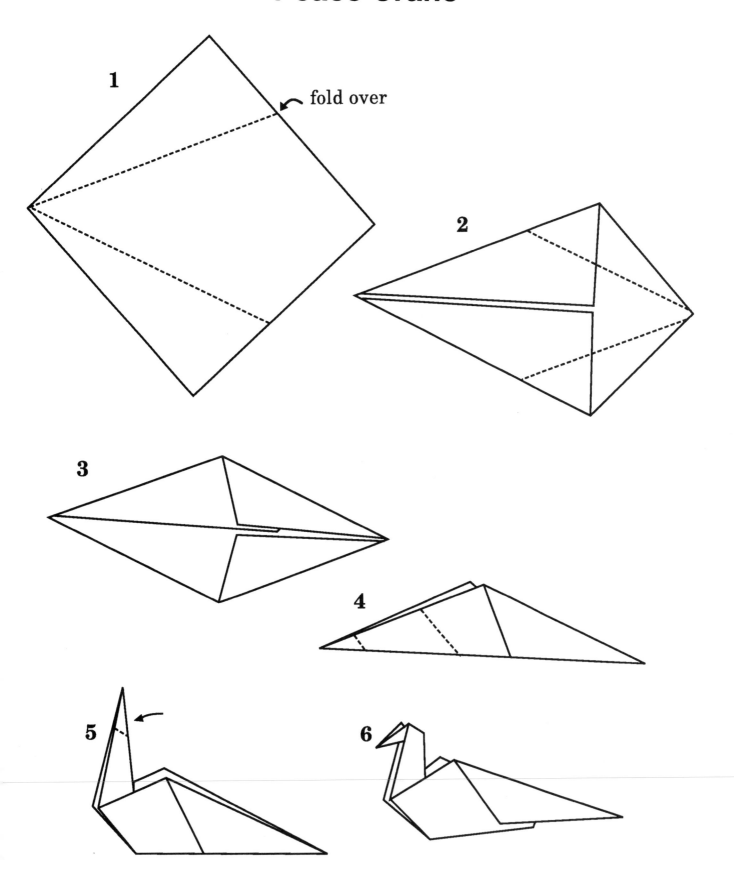

1 fold over

2

3

4

5

6

Kenya

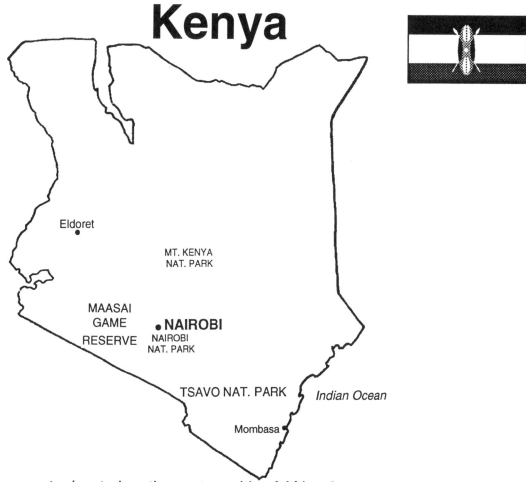

Kenya is a country located on the eastern side of Africa. Its name was derived from Mount Kenya, *Kirinyaga,* which means mountain of light. Mount Kenya is the tallest mountain in Kenya and the second highest mountain on the African continent. Most of Kenya is savana grassland but there are also fertile valleys, dry plains, dense forests, and beautiful beaches. The urban centers are quite modernized but life in small, country towns is not as developed. Two percent of the people are of Asian, Arabic or European descent. The remainder are black Africans who belong to various tribal groups. The two largest groups are the Kikuyu and the Luo. Each ethnic group has its own customs and traditions. Most have assimilated western culture while a few such as the Maasai and the Boran have strived to retain their own practices and dress. Although each group has its own language, the country's official languages are Swahili, also known as Kiswahili, and English. Zanzibar Swahili is the dialect spoken on the island of Zanzibar and along the coast of Kenya nearest the island. As one travels further north, the pronunciation and grammar change and is referred to as upcountry Swahili. Kenya's motto, *harambee,* means *pull together.* The ethnic groups in Kenya have made great efforts striving towards national unity. Some of Kenya's greatest attractions are its national parks and wildlife reserves. Ten minutes away from the modern city of Nairobi, Kenya's capital, one can tour the 28,000 acre Nairobi National Park which has more than 80 species of mammals and 500 species of birdlife. The Tsavo National Park is nearly the size of the state of Massachusetts. It has the greatest stock of wild animals in Kenya. One estimate of its elephant count is 20,000.

Word List

Numbers		
moja (mo-ja):	one	
mbili (mbee-lee):	two	
tatu (ta-too):	three	
ne (ne-nay):	four	
tano (ta-no):	five	
sita (see-ta):	six	
saba (sa-ba)	seven	
nane (na-nay):	eight	
tisa (tee-sa):	nine	
kumi (koo-mee):	ten	

Pronunciation Key

ay: as in tray; alien
y: as in by; lie; sigh
ee: as in leap; priest
u: as in dust; pun
a: as in lah dee dah
e: as in seven; rest
i: as in pin; beer; mirror
o: as in poke; loan; roam
oo: as in loony; soup
j: as in jam; giraffe
g: as in gate; again
s: as in Santa; helps
z: as in zoo; easy

Translations

asubuhi (a-soo-boo-hee):   morning
bundi (boon-dee):   owl
chai (chy):   tea
farasi (fa-ra-see):   horse
Hodi (ho-tee):   Anyone home?
Jambo (jam-bo):   hello
Karubi (ka-roo-bee):   Welcome! Come in!
Lala Salama (la-la sa-la-ma): Sleep well!
paca (pa-ka):   cat
tumbili (toom-bee-lee):   monkey, vervet

Definitions

antelope: a mammal that resembles the deer in appearance, grace, and speed, but is actually related to the cow and goat

aviary: an enclosure or cage for many birds, especially wild birds

black-bellied bustard: a large game bird; the heaviest bird (about 30 lbs.) in existence that can fly

blue touraco: a large shiny bird, the size of a turkey, with ruffled feathers found in the Kakamega Forest

Bomas of Kenya (bo-mas): a complex with traditional homesteads, artifacts, and scheduled performances of traditional dancing by various ethnic groups

cheetah: a spotted carnivore belonging to the cat family; the fastest land animal, achieving speeds of 70 m.p.h. for short durations

flying squirrel: a squirrel, extinct outside Africa, that can make long, gilding leaps through the air as far as 300 feet

gazelle: a small, swift, and graceful antelope

jackal: a wild dog about as big as a fox

Kakamega (ka-ka-may-ga): a town in western Kenya inhabited by the Luyah people

Kakamega Forest: a rain forest with open glades and grasslands where amphibians, reptiles, birds and mammals that are not seen anywhere else in Kenya can be found

Kisumu (Kee-soo-moo): a city in the province of Nyanza; a major administrative center for most of western Kenya; third largest city in Kenya

Lake Victoria: the largest lake in Africa; second largest freshwater lake in the world

Maasai (ma-sy): a nomadic cattle-herding tribe best known as East Africa's greatest warrior tribe

maize: a white large-kernel corn

mandazi (man-da-zee): deep-fried sweet dough, sometimes flavored with spices

mbira (mbir-a): an African musical instrument consisting of a hollow piece of wood with metal strips, inserted lengthwise, that vibrate when played with the thumb

Moi (mwa) **International Stadium**: Nairobi's 80,000-seat sports stadium, one of the most modern sport complexes in Africa

mongoose: a slender mammal, similar to a ferret

Nairobi (ny-ro-bee): the capital city of Kenya, located in the south central part of the country

Nakuru (na-koo-roo): Kenya's fourth largest city; its National Park hosts more than 400 species of birds

National Museum of Kenya: a museum that houses one of the world's great zoological collections; a major international center for the study of human evolution

njua (joo-a): the name given to a game played by boys in Western Province; it is called by other names such as ouri or orare, dodo and mankala in other parts of Africa

Norfolk: a historic favorite hotel in Nairobi

Nyanza (nee-an-za): capital of Western Province in Kenya

safari: a journey or trip in eastern Africa

samosa (sa-mo-sa): deep fried triangular case of chopped meat and vegetables

Snake Park: an exhibit in Nairobi of East African snakes and other reptiles

tilapia (chi-la-pee-a): a freshwater cichlid fish; an important food source in Africa

tsikora (see-kor-a): a game played by girls in Western Province in Kenya

ugali (oo-gal-ee): a mash made from maize (cornmeal) flour and water

wildebeest (wil-de-beest): an African antelope with brown stripes on its sides; both the male and female have manes, beards, and heavy down-curving horns

Kenya has several large, bustling cities. However, many native Africans live in small, remote villages. Ayuma, a young Kenyan girl, lives in Nairobi, the capital of Kenya. Andola, a young Kenyan boy, lives in a village in Western Province. For added enjoyment, divide the class so that the boys sing for Andola and the girls sing for Ayuma.

AYUMA VISITS ANDOLA
(Melody: Swing Low, Sweet Chariot)

(spoken)
Ayuma: Hodi! Hodi! Is anyone home?
Andola: Kaubi! Karubi! Come In!

Jambo! Jambo, Ayuma!
Very glad to see you here
Jambo! Jambo, Andola!
Very glad to see you, too.

Oh, won't you sit down now
and have some ugali?
Mama has been cooking all day
Asleep in the corner, see my little paca
She'll be wanting us to play.

Jambo! Jambo, Ayuma!
Very glad to see you here
Jambo! Jambo, Andola!
Very glad to see you, too.

Now, let's go outside and watch the boys
play njua
It's a game that's so much fun
I see the girls are playing tsikora
Out in the nice warm sun.

Jambo! Jambo, Ayuma!
Very glad to see you here
Jambo! Jambo, Andola!
Very glad to see you, too.

My friend has a bull to take to Kakamega
We can see bull wrestling there
We'll go to the forest;*see the blue touracos
The flying squirrel and the leopard.

Jambo! Jambo, Ayuma!
Very glad to see you here
Jambo! Jambo, Andola!
Very glad to see you, too.

*Kakamega Forest

Word List: Hodi! Karubi! Jambo! ugali, paca, njua, tsikora, Kakamega, blue touracos, flying squirrel

ANDOLA VISITS AYUMA
(Melody: Swing Low, Sweet Chariot)

(spoken)
Andola: Hodi! Hodi! Is anyone home?
Ayuma: Karibu! Karibu! Come In!

Jambo! Jambo, Andola!
Very glad to see you here
Jambo! Jambo, Ayuma!
Very glad to see you, too.

Oh, won't you sit down now
and have some samosa?
It's my favorite food to eat
Or we can have chai with a few mandazi
They are very good and sweet!

Jambo! Jambo, Andola!
Very glad to see you here
Jambo! Jambo, Ayuma!
Very glad to see you, too!

Let's go to the Norfolk; it has an aviary
We can see the beautiful birds
We'll go to the snake park;
watch them milk the snakes
Take a walk and see the flowers there.

Jambo! Jambo, Andola!
Very glad to see you here
Jambo! Jambo, Ayuma!
Very glad to see you, too!

I'd like us to go to the Bomas of Kenya
Listen to the rhythm of the drums
And then we'll go to the National Museum
And to the famous stadium.*

Jambo! Jambo, Andola!
Very glad to see you here
Jambo! Jambo, Ayuma!
Very glad to see you, too!

*Moi International Stadium

Word List: Hodi, Karubi, Jambo, mandazi, samosa, chai, Norfolk, aviary, snake park, Bomas of Kenya, National Museum

Swahili is a first or second language spoken by millions of people in Africa.

COUNTING IN SWAHILI
(Melody: Bluebird)
Moja, mbili,
Tatu, ne,
Tano, sita,
Saba, nane,
Tisa, kumi,
I'm so happy
I'm counting in Swahili

> **Word List:** *moja, mbili, tatu, ne, tano, sita, saba, nane, tisa, kumi*

ONE IS MOJA
(Melody: Paw, Paw Patch)
One is moja; two is mbili
This is how to count in Swahili
Three is tatu; four is ne (nn-nay)*
Five is tano; this is what they say

Six is sita; seven is saba
Eight is nane; nine is tisa
One more number—ten is kumi
In Swahili, you can count with me.

> **Word List:** *moja, mbili, tatu, ne, tano, sita, saba, nane, tisa, kumi*

In some parts of Kenya, the sound of the vowel "e" is spoken to rhyme with bed. In these areas, it would be sung:

Three is tatu; four is ne (nn-ne)
Five is tano; will you count, my friend?

Ugali is a daily food item for many Kenyans. It is a mash made from maize flour and water.

UGALI
(Melody: Shortenin' Bread)
Come here, dear children
Come, if you please
I will show you how to make some ugali
We need cornmeal—water, too
Stir them both together and then
Boil it through.

See ugali boiling; it's boiling, boiling
See ugali boiling; it's almost done
See ugali cooling; it's cooling, cooling
See ugali cooling now
It is done!

Come here, dear children;
Come, if you please
It is time for us to eat the ugali
Roll some 'til you make a ball
Thumbprint in the middle now
Dip it all.

Dip it in the sauce now; it's very tasty
Dip it in the sauce now; it's very good
Dip it in the sauce now; it's very tasty
I see that you like it; I knew you would.

> **Word List:** ugali

Harambee is sometimes translated as "let's pull together." It symbolizes the idea that more can be accomplished by working together than alone.

HARAMBEE*
(Melody: Kumbaya)
Harambee baba, harambee
Harambee baba, harambee
Harambee baba, harambee
Baba, harambee
Harambee mama, harambee
Harambee mama, harambee
Harambee mama, harambee
Baba, harambee
  * (Ha-ram-bay)

Substitute other names:
baba - father
mama - mother
dada - sister
kaka - brother
babu - grandfather
nyanya - grandmother
ndugu - close relative
rafiki - friend

In Kenya, visitors are invited to take a game drive. Of the forty national game parks and reserves, twenty are open to visitors. The Tsava National Park is one of the largest wildlife reserves in the world. Annually, millions of wildebeest migrate to the Maasai Mara Game Reserve. The Nairobi National Park is just eight miles out of the city of Nairobi.

SEE ALL THE ANIMALS THERE
(Melody: Rocka My Soul)

Let's take a drive and see all the animals
Let's take a drive and see all the animals
Let's take a drive and see all the animals
See all the animals there.

Go to Nairobi National Park
Go to Nairobi National Park
Go to Nairobi National Park
See all the animals there.

Antelope, hippos and black rhinoceros
Antelope, hippos and black rhinoceros
Antelope, hippos and black rhinoceros
See all the animals there.

Go to Tsavo National Park
Go to Tsavo National Park
Go to Tsavo National Park
See all the animals there.

Buffalo, cheetah, ten thousand elephants
Buffalo, cheetah, ten thousand elephants
Buffalo, cheetah, ten thousand elephants
See all the animals there.

Go to the Maasai Game Reserve
Go to the Maasai Game Reserve
Go to the Maasai Game Reserve
See all the animals there.

Wildebeest, leopards, black-bellied
bustards too
Wildebeest, leopards, black-bellied
bustards too
Wildebeest, leopards, black-bellied
bustards too
See all the animals there.

Word List: *cheetah, wildebeest, black-bellied bustards, antelope*

GOING ON A SAFARI
(Melody: Down By the Station)

Let's go to Kenya, go on a safari
I would like to see how fast
The cheetah can run
We'll see all the monkeys
Elephants and zebras
Look out lion; here I come!

Let's go to Kenya, go on a safari
I would like to see how fast
The cheetah can run
We'll see all the mongoose
Antelope and hippos
Look out lion; here I come!

Let's go to Kenya, go on a safari
I would like to see how fast
The cheetah can run
We'll see all the leopards
Buffalo and jackals
Look out lion; here I come!

Word List: *cheetah, mongoose, antelope, jackal*

This story-song is based on an African folk tale. Tribal stories are told as a means of passing on the group's heritage. Stories are often accompanied by drums or musical instruments. Songs are often incorporated into a story. Usually, the tale is an entertaining fable with a moral lesson.

TEPILIT'S SPEAR
(Melody: Joshua Fought the Battle of Jericho)
(Melody 1 is the melody of the verse; melody 2 is the melody of the refrain.)

(narrated by a Maasai elder)
A story, a story. I would like you to tell you a story—one that happened a long time ago in the village of our people. This is the story my father told.

(melody 1)	A young Maasai in Kenya Kenya, Kenya A young Maasai in Kenya Asked if he could hunt with the tribe.
(M. elder)	Now his father answered him in this way:
(melody 2)	You'll hunt the lion when you have a spear Have a spear, have a spear You'll hunt the lion when you have a spear Now go and pick some maize.

(M. elder)   So, the young Maasai, whose name was Tepilit, went to the fields to do as his father told him. As he picked maize, he noticed a root vegetable growing in the ground. Tepilit pulled it out and took it to his mother. "Mama, please cook this fine vegetable root for me," he said. Mama smiled at him and told him that she would cook the root. Tepilit left their little hut to play the mbira. When Mama had finished cooking the root, she put it in a small bowl and went looking for Tepilit. While she was gone, Tepilit's little brother saw the cooked root. It looked so very good.

(melody 1)	Now, Tepilit's brother ate the root Ate the root, ate the root Now, Tepilit's brother ate the root There was no more in the bowl.

(M. elder)   Tepilit and his mother returned to the hut and Tepilit asked his mother if he could have his root now. His mother saw that Tepilit's younger brother had eaten the root. She told Tepilit:

(melody 2)	Your brother has eaten all of it All of it; all of it Your brother has eaten all of it Here's a milk pot just for you.

(M. elder)   Well, Tepilit was very pleased to have a new milking pot. He forgot all about the root vegetable. He left the hut to find the white cow so he could fill his new pot with her milk. Tepilit walked quickly down the path. Suddenly he stopped.

melody 1)	He saw two boys who were milking goats Milking goats, milking goats He saw two boys who were milking goats But the milk leaked from their pot.

(M. elder)   There was a crack in the boys' pot. Tepilit held out his new milking pot for the boys.

89   TSD 02267-8 • *Multicultural Music*

(melody 2)   You can use my pot, but I want it back
Want it back, want it back
You can use my pot, but I want it back
Yes, I'll come back for it.

(M. elder)   Tepilit headed toward the water playing his mbira. He did not hear the crashing sound.

(melody 1)   Well, one of the boys—he dropped the pot
Dropped the pot, dropped the pot
Well, one of the boys—he dropped the pot
It was broken in tiny bits.

(M. elder)   Tepilit came back and said to them, "Please give me my pot," to which the boy who had dropped the pot replied:

(melody 2)   I can't give you your milking pot
Milking pot, milking pot
I can't give you your milking pot
But I'll give you my shiny knife.

(M. elder)   Tepilit was very pleased to have such a shiny knife. He continued on his way, until he saw his friend Kyela.

(melody 1)   Tepilit saw her cutting meat
Cutting meat, cutting meat
Tepilit saw her cutting meat
With splinters of sugar cane,

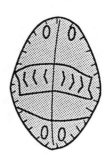

(M. elder)   He said:

(melody 2)   You can use my knife, but I want it back
Want it back, want it back
You can use my knife, but I want it back
Yes, I'll come back for it,

(M. elder)   Kyela was happy to have Tepilit's knife to cut the meat. While she cut, she hummed her favorite song. As she did, the knife cut into a bone and broke.
Just then, Tepilit returned. Kyela said to him:

(melody 1)   I can't give you your shiny knife
Shiny knife, shiny knife
I can't give you your shiny knife
I will give you my blanket,

(M. elder)   Tepilit liked the soft blanket. He thought of how warm he would be when he went to sleep that night. As he walked he noticed two warriors. They were lying on the ground. Tepilit said to them:

(melody 2)   You can use my blanket but I want it back
Want it back, want it back
You can use my blanket but I want it back
Yes, I'll come back for it,

(M. elder)   Now, the blanket wasn't big enough to cover both men. They began to fight over it. They tugged and they pulled. They pulled and tugged on it until it tore into several pieces. Tepilit came back and said to the two men, "I want my blanket now."

(melody 1)   We can't give you your blanket now
Blanket now, blanket now
We can't give you your blanket now
But we'll give you our shield.

(M. elder)   A shield! Tepilit had been given a shield! Soon Tepilit came upon a tall warrior who was hunting without a shield. He told him:

(melody 2)   You can use my shield, but I want it back
Want it back, want it back
You can use my shield, but I want it back
Yes, I'll come back for it.

(M. elder)   Tepilit sat down to play his mbira. The warrior saw a gazelle and quickly ran after it. As he ran, he fell over a big rock. The shield broke in half. He returned to Tepilit and said:

(melody 1)   I can't give back your hunting shield
Hunting shield, hunting shield
I can't give back your hunting shield
But I'll give you my spear.

(M. elder)   A spear! Tepilit was so happy! He ran all the way back to his village as fast as he could. He
shouted:

(melody 2)   Father, look; I have a spear
Have a spear, have a spear
Father, look; I have a spear
Can I go hunting now?

(M. elder)   His father replied:

(melody 2)   Yes, my son, now you can hunt
You can hunt, you can hunt
Oh yes, my son, now you can hunt
The lion in our land.

(M. elder)   Soon Tepilit went with the tribe to hunt for lion. How proud he was to have his own spear! How proud he was to be a Maasai warrior. This is the story my father told me, the story that his father told him, and his father told him. It is the story you will tell your son and he will tell his.

Note: Not too long ago, a young boy in the Maasai tribes was not considered a man until he had gone out to the grasslands and returned with a lion that he had speared.

> **Word List:** *Maasai, maize, mbira, gazelle*

Divide the class into two groups with one group singing melody 1, the verse melody and the other group singing melody 2, the refrain melody. One student is needed for the part of the Maasai elder, the narrator of the story.

Interesting facts: Maasai males are age-graded in three stages as boy, warrior and elder. Only after he has served as a warrior can a man marry. This is at approximately thirty years of age.

YOO-YOO

Not too slow

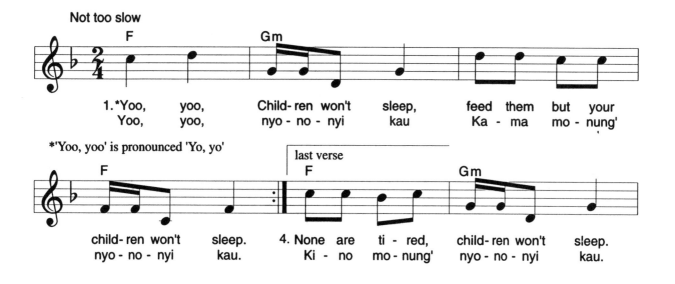

1.*Yoo,   yoo,   Child- ren won't   sleep,   feed them   but your
   Yoo,   yoo,   nyo - no - nyi   kau   Ka - ma   mo - nung'

*'Yoo, yoo' is pronounced 'Yo, yo'

child- ren won't   sleep.   4. None are   ti - red,   child- ren won't   sleep.
nyo - no - nyi   kau.   Ki - no   mo - nung'   nyo - no - nyi   kau.

Yoo,   yoo,   child- ren won't   sleep,   see them   smil - ing,
Yoo,   yoo,   nyo - no - nyi   kau   Ka - ma   mo - nung'

child- ren won't   sleep.   Who can   tire them?   child- ren won't   sleep.
nyo - no - nyi   kau   Ka - ma   mo - nung'   nyo - no - nyi   kau.

Additional English Verses:

2.   Yoo, yoo,
     Children won't sleep,
     Love them but your children won't sleep.

3.   Yoo, yoo,
     Children won't sleep,
     Hug them but your children won't sleep.

ABOT TANGEWUO

Steady

A - bot Tan - ge - wuo, coun - ting round un - til the end,
ne - ki - le ak ne - ke - le,

1 2 3 4 5 6 7 8 9 10,
Tan - ge - be ge - be mu - cho, Ngu - ngo - ro

Put your leg be - hind your Back start a - gain. stop!
ma - nya - ta chu - mbo le - co su - be cha. stop!

Make number cards to use with the song. Copy the pattern. Print the numeral on the reverse side of the card.

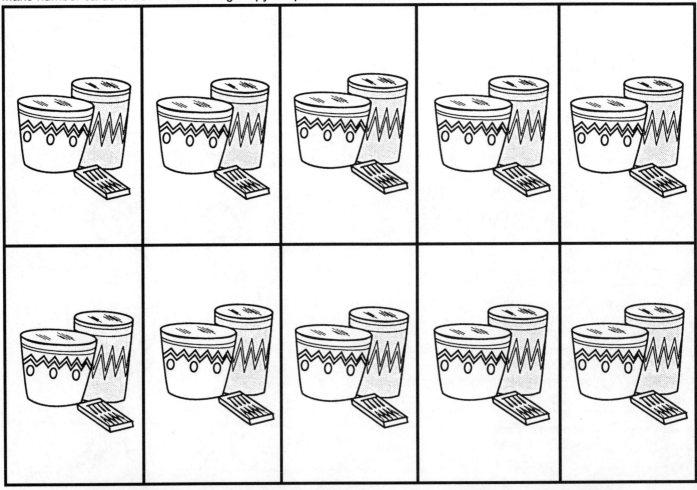

 TSD 02267-8 • *Multicultural Music*

KENYAN RECIPES

Plantain (Northern Style)
Plaintains may be boiled or sautéed in oil. To boil:
1. Cut plantain in 1-inch chunks. Add to lightly salted water and bring to a boil.
2. Cover. Reduce heat and simmer until tender. (approximately 10 minutes). Serve.

Fufu (sweet potato)
Ingredients:
3 cups sweet potatoes (cooked and mashed), 1/2 cup fine bread crumbs, 1 tsp. salt
1. Mix all ingredients.
2. Place in a skillet and cook over low heat for 10 minutes, stirring constantly.

Serve with the following stew.
Ingredients:
1 lb. cubed chicken, fish, or beef, 3 Tbsp. oil, 1 tsp. salt, 1/2 cup diced onion, 1-8 oz. can tomato sauce, 1-8 oz. can tomato paste, 1 cup water, 1 eggplant (peeled and cubed)
1. Sprinkle chicken (or fish or beef) with salt and cook over medium heat. Pieces should be lightly browned.
2. Add onion and cook until onions are golden (approximately 5 minutes).
3. Mix in tomato sauce, paste, and water. The add eggplant and cover.
4. Bring to a boil, then reduce heat and simmer until tender (approximately 30 minutes). Stir occasionally. Serve spooned over the fufu.

Fresh Fruit of the Season
Africans enjoy fresh fruit for dessert. There are over 90 varieties of bananas in Africa including some the size of one's thumb. Other fruits enjoyed by the people of Africa are: mango, papaya, tangerines, oranges, dates, guava and coconut.

Mandazi (Americanized version - doughnuts "the quick way")
Ingredients:
Refrigerated biscuits, white sugar, brown sugar or cinnamon sugar, hot oil heated in electric skillet
1. Give each student a refrigerated biscuit to pull and stretch out. Tell them to make it into a doughnut shape with a hole in the center.
2. Carefully drop each biscuit into the hot oil. Turn over so that it browns on both sides.
3. With large fork, remove "doughnut" and place it on the paper towel.
4. Sprinkle with sugar and serve warm. They taste best when served immediately.

African Chai (African tea)
Ingredients:
4 cups water, 4 bags of black tea leaves, 6 whole cardamon seeds (or powdered if seeds are not available), 3-4 cinnamon sticks, 1/2 cup sugar
1. Place the above ingredients into a large pot or kettle.
2. Bring to a boil.
3. Add 3-4 cups of whole milk or evaporated milk.
4. Bring to a boil again until it is good and hot!

African people eat **Mandazi** with their **chai.**

Activities

1. Study a map of Africa. Count the number of countries. Ask students to list the names of the countries with which they are most familiar. Which ones are in West Africa, East Africa, North Africa or South Africa? Where is Kenya in relation to the African countries they know? Obtain books on Kenya for the students to study its terrain, tribal groups, animals, languages, customs, and traditions.

2. Make stick puppets of Ayuma and Andola (page 99). Use the puppets to sing the songs *Ayuma Visits Andola* and *Andola Visits Ayuma.* Talk about the differences between city life and village life.

3. Read *Somewhere in Africa* to the class, the story about an African boy who lives in the city, wears clothes similar to their own, and has never been to the savanna grasslands of Africa to see the wild animals.

4. Serve the children mandazi and chai for snacks (see page 95 for recipes). East Africans love tea with sugar and plenty of milk. Mandazi is one of their favorite treats as well as breakfast food. The recipe found in the recipe section is a quick Americanized version that students will enjoy making.

5. Show your class pictures of African children dressed in western-style of clothing (found in library books). Also look at native costumes worn for special occasions and celebrations. Talk about the Maasai people who have chosen to wear traditional clothing daily.

6. Tell and sing the story-song in this chapter entitled "Tepilit's Spear." Use the illustrations of Tepilit, the cooked root, milking pot, knife, blanket, shield, and spear as visual aids on the felt or magnetic board. Make copies of the illustrations. Color, laminate, cut, and secure felt or magnetic tape to each piece.

7. Have the students act out the story "Tepilit's Spear," found on pages 89-91. One student can be the Maasai elder who narrates the story, one group of students can sing the lyrics written to Melody 1 and another group can sing the lyrics written to Melody 2. An accompanying drum beat can be played for each melody. Other students can pantomime the actions of the story as it is being sung by the groups or told by the narrator. Props can be used in the performance. Substitute actual items for the illustrations listed in the above activity. Have students make two drums as well as a mbira for the production.

8. Students can make drums out of coffee cans, oatmeal boxes, and other cylindrical containers. The larger the size, the deeper the sound produced. Cut a circle of thin vinyl material about one inch bigger than the container opening. Holes need to be punched 1/4 inch indented around the circumference of the circle. With the supervision of an adult, students can punch holes every 3/4 inch around the box. Lace string through the holes like the crisscross in shoe lacing. Tie very tightly to hold it well in place and for the best sound possible.

9. A mbira is a thumb piano. Throughout Africa it is called by many other names such as kalimba and sanza. Have each student bring in one plastic audio cassette tape container. Provide each student with three or four metal paper clips. These are to be unwound except for the little teardrop at the top. Place the clips at different lengths with the teardrop hanging well over the edge of the container. Tape down at the very top of the clip to hold in place. Cut a small craft stick in half. Place across the top of the row of paper clips and tape down. Wrap around the box very tightly with strong tape to hold in place. Draw a design or an African animal or village scene on the box with permanent black or brown markers.

10. Have the children make a large wall mural as a group project. Provide them with newsprint paper on which to draw mountains, savana grassland, water holes, and rain forests as well as designated areas for national parks and game reserves. Make copies of the numerous illustrations (pages 101-104) of birds and animals for them to color, cut, and paste into the various settings.

11. Pictures can be found in books at the library of the many masks that tribal groups wear for ceremonies. Students can cut the outline and eyeholes for a mask from cereal boxes. Have students collect items of nature such as twigs, leaves, straw, stones, and sand to glue onto their masks.

12. Students can design their own masks or use the illustrations provided in this chapter. Make copies of the two masks (page 92) on cardstock for them to color and cut.

13. In western Kenya, children play njua, a game for two persons. It is called by different names in other parts of Africa such as aji, awele, maa and wari. The game board is a log split in half in which 14 holes have been carved. Beans or rocks are used for the game pieces. The rules change in each region. Use egg cartons for the game board, and margarine tubs for each player's pieces. **Njua:** players sit on the opposite sides of the egg carton. Place 5 beans in each of the 12 cups of the egg carton. One player scoops up the beans from any cup in the line on his/her side of the egg carton and drops the beans one by one into the cups counterclockwise beginning with the succeeding cup until the player's hand is empty. The next player does the same. If either player drops his/her last seed into a cup on the opponent's side so that there is a total of two or three seeds in that one cup, he/she wins those seeds. The player removes them from that cup and places them in his/her margarine tub. The game continues until all the seeds are removed or neither player can play. The winner has the most seeds.

14. For more information, write or call: Embassy of the Republic of Kenya, 2249 R Street NW, Washington, DC 20008, Telephone (202) 387-6101/2/3.

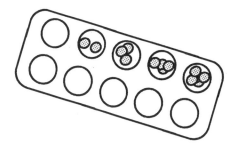

BOOKS TO READ

A is for Africa
Ife Nil Owoo
African personalities, art, and life

A is for Africa
Ifeoma Onyefulu
Village life in Africa

African Animal Tales
Rogerio Andrade Barbosa
East African fables

The Distant Talking Drum
Isaac Olaleye
A Nigerian's collection of poems recalls his small farming village

Fire on the Mountain
Jane Kurtz
An Ethiopian tale of a young boy seeking his fortune

First Book About Africa
Veronica Freman Ellis
Just Us Books

The Flying Tortoise
Tolowa M. Mollel
A Nigerian tale

Grandy the Gorilla
Jon Resnick
A day in the life of an African mountain gorilla

How the Spider Became Bald
Peter Eric Adotey Addo
Folktales and legends from West Africa

How the Turtle Got Its Shell
Sandra Robbins
An African tale

It Takes a Village
Jane Cowan Fletcher
Story based on an African proverb

Jambo Means Hello
by Tom Feelings
An East African word book

Jomo & Mata
Alyssa Chase
Two elephants come to the rescue in a savannah in East Africa

Kenya Jamo
Katherine Perrow & Virginia Overton
Life in Kenya

Land of the Four Winds
Veronica Freeman Ellis
A Liberian tale told in African dialect

The Lion's Whiskers
Nancy Raines Day
An Ethiopian folktale

Mcheshi Series:
Mcheshi Goes On A Journey
Mcheshi Goes To The Market
Mcheshi Goes To The Game Park
Sironka, Wanjku Mathenge, Okello, Otieno
Traditional and modern African life through the adventures of Mcheshi

Misoso
Verna Aardema
African cultures and traditions are portrayed in this collection of fables and folk stories

Moja Means One
by Tom Feelings
An East African counting book

My Painted House, My Friendly Chicken and Me
Maya Angelou
A young South African girl's telling of her family and life

Nobiah's Well
Donna Guthrie
An African boy helps his mother

One Round Moon for Me
Ingrid Mennen
An African boy's longing to discover his purpose in life

The Singing Man
Angela Shelf Mederaris
A tale of a Nigerian boy who leaves his West African village

Somewhere in Africa
Ingrid Mennen and Niki Daly
A story depicting the life of an African boy who lives in the city

Tales of the African Plains
retold by Anne Gatti
Twelve African folktales

Tree of Life
Barbara Bash
The Baobab tree found in the savannahs of Africa

AYUMA AND ANDOLA STICK PUPPET PATTERNS

99

TEPILIT'S SPEAR

African Animals

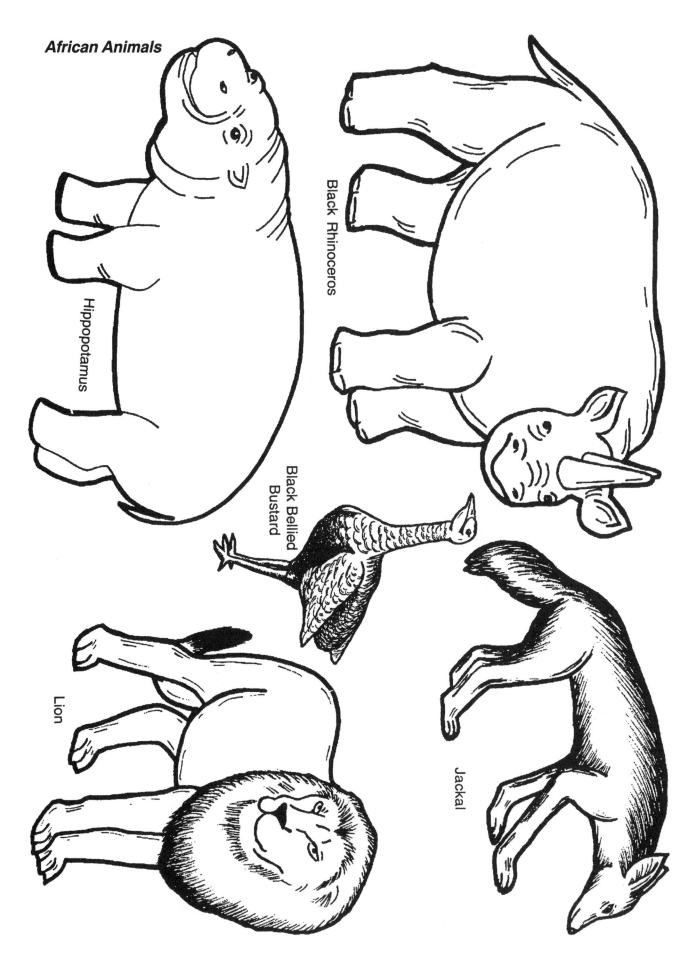

Hippopotamus

Black Rhinoceros

Black Bellied Bustard

Lion

Jackal

TSD 02267-8 • *Multicultural Music*

African Animals

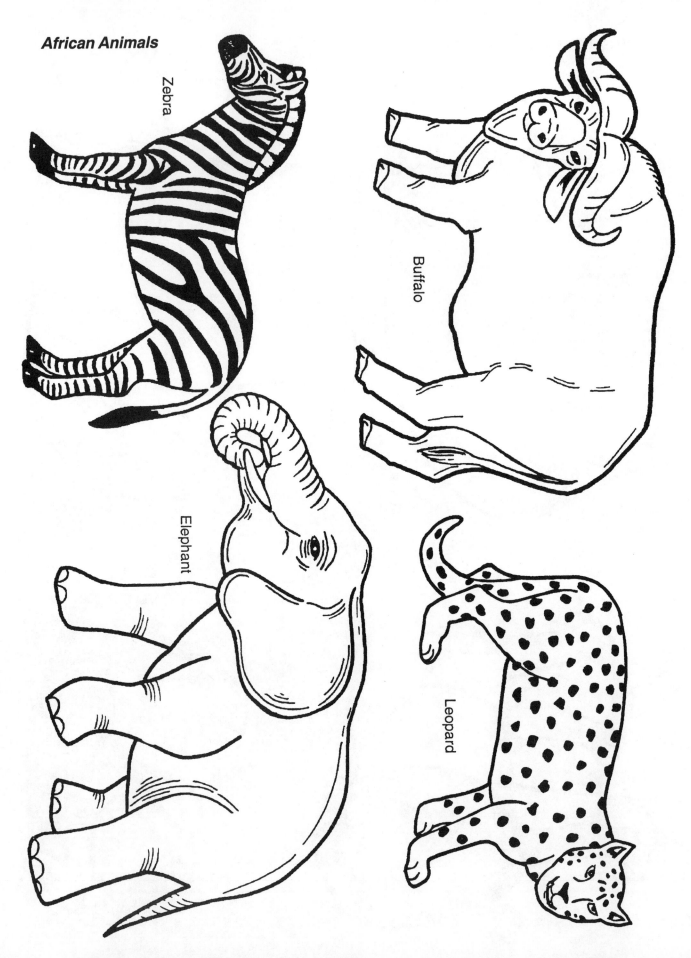

Zebra

Buffalo

Elephant

Leopard

TSD 02267-8 • *Multicultural Music*

African Animals

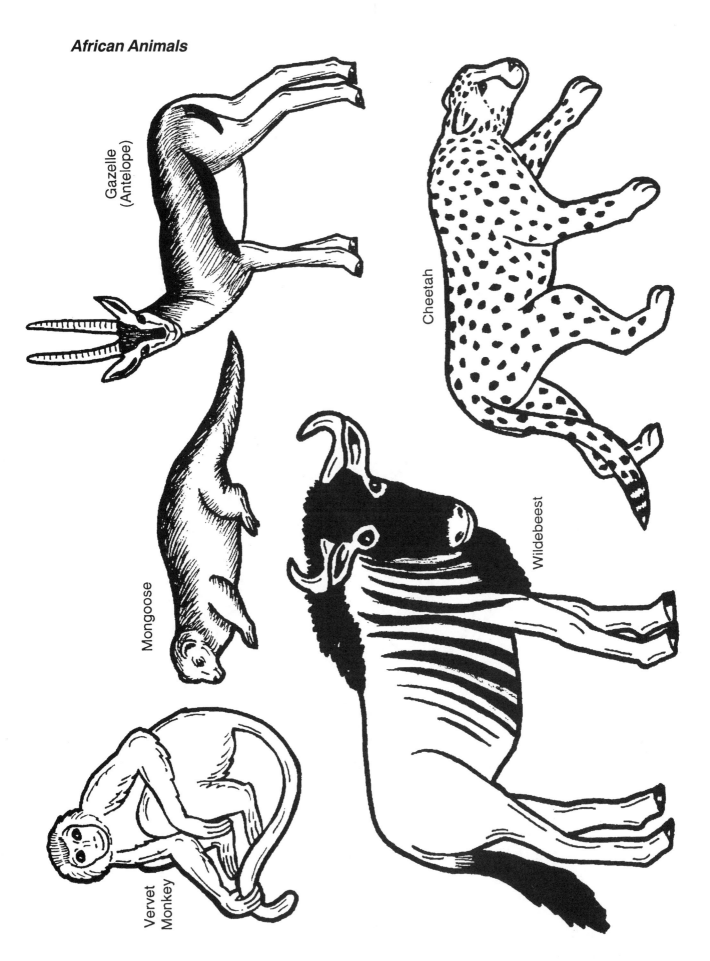

Gazelle (Antelope)

Cheetah

Mongoose

Wildebeest

Vervet Monkey

TSD 02267-8 • *Multicultural Music*

Mexico

Monterrey

Gulf of Mexico

Guadalajara

Mexico City

Sierra Madre

Mexico is a country in Latin America which borders the southwestern United States. It is a land where mountains, hills, forests, deserts and valleys are within close proximity to one another. Only one-eighth of Mexico's land is used for growing crops, yet it remains one of the world's leading producers of coffee, corn, cotton, oranges, and sugar cane. It is also a leading producer of silver. Most Mexican people are mestizos, people of mixed European and Indian ancestry. Almost all speak Spanish, the official language of Mexico; many Mexican Indians also speak an Indian language. Mexico City is the capital of Mexico and the largest city in the world. There one can see Aztec Indian ruins and beautiful palaces of the past as well as modern skyscrapers. Places to visit are the Zócalo, where the emperor's palace and the Great Temple once stood, the National Cathedral, the National Pawnshop, the National Theatre, and the Paseo de la Reforma, one of the most beautiful boulevards in the world. Another attraction is the popular sport, jai alai which is sometimes called the fastest game in the world. It is similar to handball. Holidays are celebrated with festivals called fiestas. There is dancing, entertainment, and plenty of food and drink. The highlights are the parades and the early morning and late evening fireworks.

WORD LIST

Animals

burrito (boo-ree-to):	little burro or little donkey
burro (boo-ro):	donkey
caballito (ka-ba-yee-to):	little horse; pony
caballo (ka-by-yo):	horse
gansito (gan-see-to):	gosling
ganso (gan-so):	goose
gatito (ga-tee-to):	kitten
gato (ga-to):	cat
patito (pa-tee-to):	duckling
pato (pa-to):	duck
perrito (per-ree-to):	puppy
perro (per-ro):	dog
pollito (po-yee-to):	chick
pollo (poy-yo):	hen
torrito (tor-ree-to):	young bull
torro (tor-ro):	bull
vaquito (va-kee-to):	calf
vaca (va-ka):	cow

Pronunciation Key

ay: as in t**ray**; **a**lien
y: as in b**y**; l**ie**; s**igh**
ee: as in l**ea**p; pr**ie**st
u: as in d**u**st; p**u**n
a: as in l**a**h dee dah
e: as in s**e**ven; r**e**st
i: as in p**i**n; b**ee**r; m**i**rror
o: as in p**o**ke; l**oa**n; r**oa**m
oo: as in l**oo**ny; s**ou**p
j: as in **j**am; **gi**raffe
g: as in **g**ate; a**g**ain
s: as in **S**anta; help**s**
z: as in **z**oo; ea**s**y

Numbers

uno (oo-no):	one
dos (dos):	two
tres (trays):	three
cuatro (kwa-tro):	four
cinco (seen-ko):	five
seis (says):	six
siete (see-e-tay):	seven
ocho (o-cho):	eight
nueve (noo-ay-bay):	nine
diez (dee-ays):	ten

Translations

aqui (a-kee):	here
Buenos Dias (bway-nas dee-as):	Good Day
Buenos Noces (bway-nos no-chays):	Good Night
Maria (Ma-ree-a):	Mary
muchacha (moo-cha-cha):	girl
muchacho (moo-cha-cho):	boy
Ole! (o-lay):	Bravo!
Pedro (pay-dro):	Peter
por favor (por fa-vor):	please
Si (see):	yes
el torro (el tor-ro):	bull
Vengan (bayn-gan):	Come
Vengan aqui (bayn-gan a-kee)	Come here
Viva Mexico (vee-va mee-hee-ko):	Long live Mexico

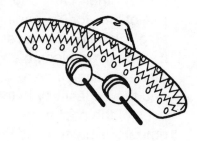

Definitions

arroz con leche (a-roz kon lay-chay): rice with milk

bongo: a small drum held between the knees, especially used in Latin America and Africa

castanets: one of a pair of instruments shaped like small cymbals, held in the hand and clicked together; usually from wood or ivory

Cinquo de Mayo (seen-ko day my-yo): the fifth of May; a holiday

clave (kla-vay): one of a pair of rounded wooden sticks, struck together as rhythmic accompaniment

enchilada (ayn-chi-la-da): a tortilla rolled up and filled with chopped meat, chicken, or cheese and covered with a hot sauce

fiesta (fee-es-ta): a festival or celebration

flan (flan): a dessert of smooth custard topped with caramel syrup

guiro (gwir-o): a notched gourd used as a musical instrument in Latin America

maracas (ma-ra-kas): seeds or pebbles enclosed in a dried gourd and shaken like a rattle; usually played in pairs

mariachi (ma-ree-a-chee): strolling musicians

peso (pay-so): Mexican dollar

piñata (peen-nya-ta): a container made of earthenware or papier-mâché (often in the shape of an animal) which is filled with treats (candy, fruit, toys). A piñata is hung above the heads of children who take turns trying to break it with a stick while blindfolded. After it breaks, they scramble for the treats that have fallen out.

poncho (pon-cho): large piece of cloth with a slit for the head; worn in South America as a cloak

rebozo (ray-bo-zo): long, wide scarf worn by women and girls

salsa (sal-sa): a sauce made with fresh tomatoes, onion, cilantro, and peppers

sarape (sa-ra-pay): blanket which men use as a scarf or cloak

Sierra Madre (see-er-ra ma-dray): series of mountain ranges in Mexico

sombrero (som-brer-o): broad-brimmed hat, usually made of straw

tacitos (ta-kee-tos): small tacos

tacos (ta-kos): a folded tortilla filled with chopped meat, chicken, or cheese

tamale (ta-ma-lay):Mexican food made of corn meal and ground meat seasoned with red peppers, wrapped in corn husks and roasted or steamed

tostadas (tos-ta-das): a deep-fried tortilla served flat with beans, cheese, lettuce, meat, and onions on the top

tortilla (tor-tee-ya): thin flat pancake made of corn meal

A feature of Mexican small town life is the open-air market where people of the surrounding country-side bring their fruit, vegetables, blankets, and pottery to sell or barter. Often there is a small orchestra to add to the gaiety. Strolling musicians, called mariachi, wander about town to play requested songs for a fee. Mariachi music is known throughout the world and has come to symbolize Mexico.

LET'S GO TO MEXICO
(Melody: When The Saints Go Marching In)

Oh here we go—we're on the road
We're on our way to Mexico
Oh we will see the Sierra Madre
When we go to Mexico!

We'll eat the food—Mexican food
Some hot tamales, beans and rice
I'd like to have arroz con leche
And some flan would be real nice!

Let's shop today— it's market day
We'll bargain for a big sombrero
I'll buy a nice rebozo and poncho
Some maracas and a guiro.

Hear the guitars and violins
The bass and horns are playing, too
Just give the mariachis some pesos
And they'll play a song for you.

See the parade—the big parade
The people come and celebrate
The fifth of May is Cinquo de Mayo
It's a great fiesta day!

Oh here we go—back on the road
It's time to leave old Mexico
Oh, we can hear the sounds of the children
Shouting "Viva Mexico"!

> **Word List:** Sierra Madre, tamales, arroz con leche, flan, sombrero, rebozo, poncho, maracas, guiro, mariachis, pesos, Cinquo de Mayo, fiesta, Viva Mexico!

In the Mexican diet, the basic food is corn. Thin corn meal pancakes called tortillas are served like bread with every meal. The tortilla can be folded, filled and served with or without sauce as a taco, tostada, or enchilada.

PEDRO AND MARIA
(Melody: La Cucaracha)

His name is Pedro
His name is Pedro
He was born in Mexico
He's a muchacho
He's a muchacho
Guadalupe is his home!

He eats tostadas
He eats tostadas
Fried tortilla, beans and cheese
He likes tostadas
He likes tostadas
Pass the salsa, if you please.

See his sombrero
See his sombrero
Pedro wears it every day!
His big sombrero
His big sombrero
Keeps the sun and rain away.

Her name's Maria
Her name's Maria
She was born in Mexico
She's a muchacha
She's a muchacha
Guadalupe is her home!

She eats tacitos
She eats tacitos
Soft tortilla filled with meat
She likes tacitos
She likes tacitos
It's her favorite food to eat!

See her rebozo
See her rebozo
Maria wears it every day!
Her nice rebozo
Her nice rebozo
Keeps her nice and warm—Ole!

> **Word List:** Pedro, Maria, muchacho, muchacha, tostadas, tortilla, salsa, sombrero, tacitos, rebozo, Ole!

About 297 million people in the world speak Spanish. It is the most popular of the Romance languages which include French, Italian, and Portugese. The Spanish spoken in Mexico is called American Spanish. It is basically the same as the Spanish spoken in Spain, Castilian Spanish, with a few differences in pronunciation and vocabulary.

WHAT IS A GATO?
(Melody: Chiapanecas)

What is a gato? A cat! A cat!*
What is a gato? A cat! A cat!
What is a perro? A dog! A dog!
What is a perro? A dog! A dog!
Sing, sing! Sing now in Spanish!
Sing, sing! Sing now in English!
Sing now—sing a song
With new words from our Mexican friends—Ole!

What is a pato? A duck! A duck!
What is a pato? A duck! A duck!
What is a pollo? A chicken! A chicken!
What is a pollo? A chicken! A chicken!
Sing, sing! Sing now in Spanish!
Sing, sing! Sing now in English!
Sing now—sing a song
With new words from our Mexican friends—Ole!

What is a ganso? A goose! A goose!
What is a ganso? A goose! A goose!
What's a caballo? A horse! A horse!
What's a caballo? A horse! A horse!
Sing, sing! Sing now in Spanish!
Sing, sing! Sing now in English!
Sing now—sing a song
With new words from our Mexican friends—Ole!

What's Buenos Dias? Good Day! Good Day!
What's Buenos Dias? Good Day! Good Day!
What's Buenos Noces? Good Night! Good Night!
What's Buenos Noces? Good Night! Good Night!
Sing, sing! Sing now in Spanish!
Sing, sing! Sing now in English!
Sing now—sing a song
With new words from our Mexican friends—Ole!

Word List: *gato, perro, pato, pollo, ganso, caballo, Buenos Dias, Buenos Noces, Ole!*

---

*Variation: instead of repeating the name of the animal, sing the animal's sound, i.e. "What is a gato? A cat! Meow!" Continue in this manner throughout the song.

THE ANIMALS ON MY FARM
(Melody: Pretty Little Dutch Girl)

I had a cute gatito
My daddy gave to me
But now he is a gato 'cause
He grew up big you see!

I had a cute perrito
My daddy gave to me
But now he is a perro 'cause
He grew up big you see!

I had a cute patito
My daddy gave to me
But now he is a pato 'cause
He grew up big you see!

I had a cute pollito
My daddy gave to me
But now he is a pollo 'cause
He grew up big you see!

I had a cute burrito
My daddy gave to me
But now he is a burro 'cause
He grew up big you see!

I had a cute gansito
My daddy gave to me
But now he is a ganso 'cause
He grew up big you see!

Additional Choices:
torrito, torro
caballito, caballo

Word List: *gatito, gato, perrito, perro, patito, pato, pollito, pollo, burrito, burro, gansito, ganso, torrito, torro, caballito, caballo*

YO CUENTO (I Am Counting)
Melody: Three Blind Mice

Uno, dos, tres	(echo)
Cuatro, cinquo, seis	(echo)
Siete, ocho, nueve, diez	(echo)
Yo cuento.	(echo)

Divide the class into two groups: boys and girls, left and right sides of the class, or counting off by twos. Repeating the song in various ways increases fun and learning.

109

The Mexican people love music, dancing, and singing. The instruments in this song are available to tourists in Mexico. They are also sold in music stores and some toy stores in the United States.

LET'S MAKE MUSIC, MUCHACHOS
(Melody: La Bamba)

Bam-ba, bamba
Bam-ba, bamba
Bam-ba, bamba

Hey, muchachos, let's make music
Hey, muchachas, let's make music
Come everyone, come join the fun
Come join the fun!
Bam-ba, bamba
Bam-ba, bamba
Bam-ba, bamba

Now, let's hear from the claves
Now, let's hear from the claves
Come everyone, come join the fun
Come join the fun
Bam-ba, bamba
Bam-ba, bamba
Bam-ba, bamba

Now let's hear from the guiros
Now let's hear from the guiros
Come everyone, come join the fun
Come join the fun
Bam-ba, bamba
Bam-ba, bamba
Bam-ba, bamba

Now let's hear the maracas
Now let's hear the maracas
Come everyone, come join the fun
Come join the fun
Bam-ba, bamba
Bam-ba, bamba
Bam-ba, bamba

Now, let's hear from the bongos
Now, let's hear from the bongos
Come everyone, come join the fun
Come join the fun
Bam-ba, bamba
Bam-ba, bamba
Bam-ba, bamba
Bamba!

Word List: *muchachos, muchachas, claves, guiros, maracas, bongos*

The piñata comes in many shapes and sizes. The most popular choices are the burrito (young burro) and the torrito (young bull).

THE PIÑATA
(Melody: Mama Paquito)

Time for fiesta—Time for fiesta
Tell the children that we have a game to play
Time for fiesta—Time for fiesta
There will be treats for each of them to have today!

See the piñata—See the piñata
A torrito trimmed with paper green and blue
See the piñata—See the piñata
It's filled with treats and toys for everyone of you!

Break the piñata—Break the piñata
You can hear the children as they start to shout
Break the piñata—Break the piñata
We want the candy and the toys to all fall out!

Pick up the treats now—Pick up the treats now
There are toys and candies and some pennies, too
Pick up the treats now—Pick up the treats now
Little torrito has been very good to you!

Word List: *fiesta, torrito, piñata*

The Mexican Hat Dance is the national dance of Mexico. Teach the children to sing the Mexican Hat Dance Song on this page. Next, demonstrate the dance while they sing the song. Then teach the children the dance using the Instruction Song on this page. After the children have learned the steps well, eliminate the words of the Instruction Song and join them in singing and dancing the Mexican Hat Dance Song.

MEXICAN HAT DANCE SONG
(Melody: Mexican Hat Dance)

There is a famous dance	*(clap, clap)*
They do in Mexico	*(clap, clap)*
And when they do this dance	*(clap, clap)*
I'm sure that you will know	*(clap, clap)*

You go 'round and around in a circle
Around the sombrero you go
Everyone, everywhere loves it
The hat dance of old Mexico

INSTRUCTION SONG
(Melody: Mexican Hat Dance)

Right heel, left heel, right heel	*(clap, clap)*
Now left, then right, now left	*(clap, clap)*
Right heel, left heel, right heel	*(clap, clap)*
Now left, then right, now left	*(clap, clap)*

Hold hands and go round in a circle
(or Lock arms and go round in a circle)*
Go round the sombrero and stop
The other way round in a circle
Keep going around, now you stop!

Instructions:

A. Individuals form a large circle around a large sombrero or partners face each other*
B. Each participant places his/her hands on his/her hips
C. Jump while changing feet, i.e. right heel back and left heel forward at the same time.
    Jump while changing feet again, i.e. left heel back and right heel forward at the same time.
D. Hold hands or lock arms and circle to the left and then to the right.

*Younger children may form a large circle and do the dance; they can join hands when it is time to "go 'round in a circle." Older children may interlock arms at the elbows with partners to go around in small circles.

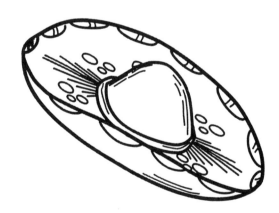

CABALLITO BLANCO
(Mexican folk song)

Level: U and L
Key of C: start Em

Ca - bal - li - to   blan - co   sa - ca - me de_a - qui___

Lle - va - me_a mi   pueb - lo   don - de - yo   na - ci___

2. Tengo, tengo, tengo, tu no tienes nada
Tengo tres borregas en una manada.

3. Una me da leche, otra me da lana
Y otra mantequilla para le semana.

English translation:
White Horse take me away from here
Take me to the town where I was born
I have, I have, I have
You don't have anything
I have three lambs in a flock
One gives me milk, the other gives me wool
And the third one gives me butter
for the whole week.

       TSD 02267-8 • *Multicultural Music*

LOS POLLITOS
(The Little Chicks)

Los po - lli - tos di - cen pí - o, pí - o pí - o
La ga - lli - na bus - ca el ma - íz y_el tri - go,
Ba - jo sus dos a - las, a - cu - rru - ca - di - tos,

cuan - do tie - nen ham - bre, cuan - do tie - nen frí - o.
les da la co - mi - da, y les pres - ta_a - bri - go.
has - ta_el o - tro dí - a, duer - man los po - lli - tos.

THE LITTLE CHICKS
(Los Pollitos)

Lit - tle chicks are call-ing, pi - o, pi - o, pi - o,
Mo - ther hen goes look-ing for grains of wheat and corn to
All a - round their mo-ther the chicks are snug-gled near. Be -

when they need to eat or when they're feel-ing cold.
feed them for their din - ner and she keeps them warm.
neath her wings they sleep 'till a - no - ther day is here.

114

MI RANCHO

Ven - gan a ver mi_____ que_es her - mo_____ sa. Ven - gan a ver mi_

____ que_es her - mo_____ sa El pa - ti - to ha - ce_a -

sí, cuá, cuá. El pa - ti - to ha - ce_a - sí, cuá, cuá, Ven -

gan ca - ma - rade, ven - gan ca - ma - rade, ven - gan, ven - gan, ven - gan. Ven -

gan ca - ma - rade, ven - gan ca - ma - rade, ven gan, ven - gan, ven - gan.

Come to see my farm
for it is beautiful (sing twice)
The duck goes like this, quack, quack. (sing twice)

Chorus:
Oh, come, my friends,
Oh, come, my friends,
Oh, come to see my farm.

Repeat the song, replacing the verse in boldface with one of the following verses.

El pollito hace así, pío, pío.
La vaquita hace así, mú, mú.
El puerquito hace así, oinc, oinc.
El burrito hace así, íja, íja.
El gallito hace así, kikiri, kí.
El perrito hace así, guau, guau.
El gatito hace así, miau, miau.

The chick goes like this, peep, peep.
The cow goes like this, moo, moo.
The pig goes like this, oink, oink.
The donkey goes like this, hee-haw, hee-haw.
The rooster goes like this, cock-a-doodle-doo.
The dog goes like this, bow wow.
The cat goes like this, meow, meow.

MEXICAN HAT DANCE
(La Raspe)

THE ADVENTURE OF THE CURIOUS ANIMALS
A Picture Board Story for the Flannel or Magnetic Board

Material needed: 1 board (flannel or magnetic)
Animal Pictures: 1 burrito, 2 burros, 1 pato, 1 patito, 1 perrito, 1 perro, 1 caballo, 1 gatito, el torro
The following are optional: 1 farmhouse, 1 pond, 1 large barn, 1 old shabby barn (shapes cut from construction paper), plus 1 pollo and 1 pollito to be placed by large barn

One morning little Burrito decided that she would take a long, long walk. She wanted to explore Señor Eduardo's farmyard. Papa Burro and Mama Burro were still asleep. So, as quietly as she could, little Burrito left Señor Eduardo's barn and started down the path toward the pond where Mama Pato and little Patito were splashing. As Burrito strolled along, little Perrito came running out onto the grassy meadow and barked, "Where are you going, little Burrito? Can I go, too?" Before little Burrito could answer, Mama Perro came barking very loudly, telling her little Perrito to get right back where he belonged.

Little Burrito continued on her way. Señor Eduardo's farm was so big and little Burrito had never walked so far before. In the pasture she could see Caballo. Quickly, she raced over to him. "Venga, Caballo, venga! Come! Come with me! We will go on an adventure." Caballo liked adventures. So off he galloped with Burrito to explore the big farmyard. Soon Burrito and Caballo came to an old wooden building. "What is this here?" hee-hawed little Burrito.

"I don't know," whinnied Caballo. "Let's find the door," he said, as he trotted off to the other side of the shabby building. "The door is locked," said Caballo with a neigh.

"I see a window," brayed little Burrito. "Maybe we can take a look inside!"

"The window is so very high," Caballo told Burrito as they came closer and took another look. "Perhaps, if you climb up on my back you will be able to see inside."

Little Burrito climbed up on Caballo's back and tried to steady herself as best as she could. "I can't see inside!" she hee-hawed. At that moment, little Perrito came barking around the corner.

"Let me see! Let me see!" he barked.

"Venga aca! Venga aca! Come here, Perrito," said Caballo who was standing as still as he could so that little Burrito would not fall. "See if you can jump way up on Burrito's back. Then you will be able to look in the window and tell us what you see!"

Perrito barked happily! He liked to jump high and he was very curious as to what he might see in this old barn. Up, up, up, Perrito jumped! But he did not jump high enough! Up, up, up, again he tried!

"Por favor, Perrito. Please! Please try again!" brayed little Burrito! Perrito tried once more to jump as high as he could. This time he landed right on Burrito's back! All three animals quivered and shook! "You did it!" shouted Burrito.

"We almost fell over," groaned Caballo!

"What do you see?" asked little Burrito.

Perrito barked, "I cannot see inside." Perrito stretched. He stretched himself as much as he could until his nose touched the bottom of the window pane. "Almost," he barked. "I can almost see inside!"

"Meow! Meow!"

"What's that? What do I hear down there?" asked Perrito, almost falling off Burrito's back.

"It's Gatito," cried Burrito! "I hear Gatito! Maybe she can see in the window!"

Caballo called, "Venga aca! Venga aca! Come here, little Gatito!"

"Meow," cried Gatito. "What are you doing?"

"We're having an adventure!" Caballo neighed. "We are trying to look in the window so that we can see what's inside this old barn! Can you help us? Can you climb to the top?"

"Meow!" cried Gatito. "I will!" She loved the idea of climbing up on Caballo's back, then onto Burrito's back, and then onto Perrito's back.

"Be careful," Burrito called out as Gatito reached the very top!

"I will," Gatito meowed.

At that moment Burrito began to quiver, "I think I'm going to sneeze," she cried out!

Just as Burrito spoke, Gatito turned her head to see something coming toward them! "El torro!" she cried. "El torro!" she cried again as she jumped off Perrito and landed on Caballo who reared up and gave a loud whinny! At that, all the animals came tumbling down in a big heap! "El torro! El torro!" Gatito cried again as she quickly hurried back to Señor Eduardo's farmhouse! Caballo, Burrito, and Perrito got up as quickly as they could and hurried off.

"El torro! El torro!" they echoed, as they headed back. They had had enough adventure. Finding out what was in the shabby old barn would have to wait for another day!

Arroz con Leche (Rice Pudding)

Ingredients:

2 quarts milk, 1 can sweetened condensed milk, 1 Tbsp. butter, 1 cup rice, 1 1/2 cups sugar, 1 cinnamon stick, 3 egg yolks

1. Boil 1 quart of milk with cinnamon stick in a saucepan, remove from heat.
2. Add rice and leave soaking for 2 hours.
3. Cook and add the rest of the hot milk as needed.
4. When the rice is very soft, remove from heat and add the sugar, condensed milk, beaten egg yolks, and butter.
5. Place over heat to thicken.
6. Let mixture cook and sprinkle with cinnamon.

Bunuelos (Fried Sweet Puffs)

Ingredients:

1/2 cup water, 2 Tbsp. packed brown sugar, 1 egg, slightly beaten, 2 Tbsp. butter, 2 cups all-purpose flour, 1/2 tsp. baking powder, vegetable oil, sugar, cinnamon, honey

1. Heat water and brown sugar in a 1-quart saucepan to a boil; boil uncovered for 2 minutes.
2. Cool; stir in egg. Cut butter into flour, baking powder, and salt until mixture resembles fine crumbs.
3. Stir in egg mixture.
4. Turn dough onto lightly floured surface. Knead until elastic, about 5 minutes.
5. Shape dough into roll, 20 inches long.
6. Cover and let rest 1 hour.
7. Heat oil (1 inch) to 365°.
8. Cut dough into 1-inch slices, roll each slice on a lightly floured surface into a 5-inch circle.
9. Fry circles, turning once, until golden brown (about 2 minutes).
10. Drain on paper towels.
11. Sprinkle with sugar and cinnamon or serve with honey.
    Yields 20 fried puffs.

Flan (Custard)

Ingredients:

3/4 cup sugar, 2 Tbsp. water, 1/2 cup sugar, 2 eggs (slightly beaten), 1/2 tsp. vanilla, 1/4 tsp. ground nutmeg, 1/4 tsp. ground cinnamon, 1/4 tsp. ground allspice, 2 cups milk (scalded, then cooled)

1. Heat 3/4 cup sugar in heavy 1-quart saucepan over low heat, stirring constantly, until sugar is melted and golden brown.
2. Gradually stir in water. Divide syrup evenly among six 6-ounce custard cups.
3. Allow syrup to harden in cups about 10 minutes.
4. Mix 1/2 cup sugar, eggs, vanilla, nutmeg, cinnamon, and allspice. Gradually stir in scalded milk.
5. Pour custard mixture over syrup.
6. Place cups in rectangular pan (13" x 9" x 2") on oven rack.
7. Pour very hot water into pan to within 1/2 inch of tops of cups.
8. Bake in 350° oven until knife inserted halfway between center and edge comes out clean, about 45 minutes.
9. Remove cups from water.
10. Refrigerate until chilled; unmold at serving time.
    Six servings.

Queso Asado (Baked Cheese)

Ingredients:

1 cup shredded Cheddar cheese (about 4 oz.), 1 cup shredded Muenster cheese (about 4 oz.), 1 cup shredded mozzarella cheese (about 4 oz.), 1 spiced sausage cooked and cut into 6 slices

1. Mix cheeses; divide mixture among six ungreased 6-ounce custard cups.
2. Top each with sausage.
3. Place cups on cookie sheet. Cook uncovered in 350° oven until cheese is melted, about 15 minutes.
4. Serve with tortilla chips if desired.

Chile con Queso (Chile with Cheese)

Ingredients:

1 cup shredded Cheddar or Monterey Jack cheese (about 4 oz.), 1 can (4 oz.) chopped green chilies, drained, 1/4 cup half-and-half, 2 Tbsp. finely chopped onion, 2 tsp. ground cumin.

1. Heat all ingredients over low heat, stirring constantly, until cheese is melted.
2. Serve with tortilla chips if desired.

Entomados de Queso (Red Enchiladas with Cheese)

Ingredients:

1 cup finely chopped onion, 2 cloves garlic, finely chopped, 1 cup vegetable oil, 1 cup chicken broth, 8 tomatoes, chopped, 1 Tbsp. chili powder, 1 tsp. salt, 1 tsp. ground cumin, 1 tsp. dried oregano leaves, 12 corn or flour tortillas, 3 cups shredded cheese (about 12 oz.), sour cream

1. Cook and stir onion and garlic in oil in 12-inch skillet over medium heat until onion is tender.
2. Stir in chicken broth, tomatoes, chili powder, salt, cumin, and oregano, heat to boiling; reduce heat. Simmer uncovered 1 hour.
3. Dip each tortilla into sauce to coat both sides.
4. Spoon 2 tablespoons of the cheese onto each tortilla; roll tortilla around filling.
5. Place seam side down in ungreased rectangular baking dish (13" x 9" x 2").
6. Pour remaining sauce over enchiladas; sprinkle with remaining cheese.
7. Cook uncovered in 350° oven until cheese is melted, about 15 minutes.
8. Serve with sour cream.

Chocolate Caliente

Ingredients:

3 oz. unsweetened chocolate, 1/2 cup sugar, 1 tsp. cinnamon, 6 cups milk, 2 eggs (beaten), 2 tsp. vanilla

1. Mix chocolate, sugar, cinnamon, and 1 cup milk in large saucepan over medium heat. Stir until chocolate melts.
2. Add remaining milk.
3. Remove 1 cup of hot chocolate mixture and add to the beaten eggs, stirring constantly.
4. Quickly add the egg/chocolate mixture to the hot chocolate in the saucepan.
5. Heat for 2 minutes, then remove from heat and use a hand-held mixer to beat in vanilla until frothy. Serve plain or with whipped cream and cinnamon sticks.

Projects and Activities

1. Use the Mexican boy and girl provided as visual aids for the song, *Pedro and Maria*. Copy, color, cut, and laminate the figures (patterns found on pages 124-125), clothing, accessories, and food items. Put magnetic or felt tape on the backs of all items. Place the tape on the edges of the rebozo, poncho, and sombrero so that these can be placed on top of the figures as you sing the appropriate lines in the song. Place the tostadas and tacitos on the board as these are sung in the song. Talk about these food dishes as well as the tortillas and enchiladas. All of these items are defined in the word list section.

2. The animal picture cards (patterns found on pages 126-127) can be used as visual aids for the three songs: *What Is A Gato?*, *The Animals on My Farm*, and *How Many Baby Animals?*

3. The children can dramatize the song, *The Animals on My Farm*. Paste a copy of Pedro (page 125) on a 9" by 12" sheet of construction paper. Do the same with a copy of Maria (page 124). Punch holes and attach yarn at the top of the cards so a child can wear it around the neck. Make copies of the animals that are listed in the song. Color, cut, and laminate each animal and tape individually onto craft sticks. Children can take turns as Pedro and Maria. They will each select a verse to sing with the corresponding baby and adult animal to show.

4. Make a memory game. Photocopy two sets of cards featuring the animals. Color and laminate. The children can use them to play a memory match game.

5. Students can make an animal picture dictionary. Make copies of the animals so that each student has a set. Provide students with 4 sheets of 9" by 12" paper. Instruct each to cut the paper into quarters and staple them together at the top or left side to make a booklet. They will then cut the picture squares and paste each animal in their booklet in alphabetical order. Students can elect to color the animals and print their English translation on each page. Have the students read the vocabulary in their animal picture dictionary as a group. This is an opportunity to practice the Spanish words.

6. Teach the song, *The Piñata*. Have the students make a piñata. Instructions and illustrations are included on page 123. Display the piñata until Mexican Fiesta Day. Play the piñata game. The piñata is hung from the ceiling. Children take turns striking it while blindfolded until the piñata breaks open and the treats within spill out.

7. Create a mariachi band using percussion instruments. Obtain bongos, maracas, claves, and guiros. Students can take turns playing these musical instruments as the class sings, *Let's Make Music Muchachos* (page 110).

8. Have a Mexican Fiesta on the day of your choice or celebrate the Mexican holiday, *Cinquo de Mayo* on May 5th. Offer parents the Mexican recipes in this chapter and ask them to prepare these or other favorite Mexican dishes. Sing the songs provided while students take turns using percussion instruments to add to the merriment. Play the piñata game. Sing and dance the *Mexican Hat Dance Song*, located on page 111.

9. Tell the story, *The Adventure of the Curious Animals* (pages 117-118) using the animal pictures (pages 126-127) on a magnetic or felt board. Point to each animal as you use its Spanish name in the story.

10. Make guiros. Collect 12 oz. frozen juice cans. Cut corrugated cardboard into sizes to fit around each can. Students can glue the cardboard around the cans. Provide each student with an unsharpened pencil to scrape the guiro rhythmically as the class sings a Mexican song. The guiros must be very dry before they can be played.

11. Students can play "OLE!" They will learn to count and read numbers in Spanish and recognize the Mexican flag.

    OLE! —a fun way to learn numbers in Spanish
    Number of players: four

Equipment needed: 2 sets of Spanish number cards, cars with Mexican flag, card with "Mexico" written on it, 4 cups, 1 Mexican Bean Bowl (a bowl labeled "Mexico" filled with 160 pinto beans). Each of the four players can drop ten beans into the bowl four times, as they count in Spanish.

Preparation: Place the Mexican Bean Bowl in the center of the playing area. Shuffle the Spanish number cards and place them face down to the left of the bean bowl. Give one cup to each player.

Play: Players take turns drawing number cards from the center pile. Each player reads aloud the number drawn and places the card, face up, in a discard pile to the right of the Mexican Bean Bowl. The player removes the correct number of beans from the bowl, counting aloud in Spanish. These beans are placed in the player's cup. If a player draws the Mexican flag, all other players shout "Ole!" The card is placed in the discard pile and 5 beans must be removed from the player's cup or the amount that is in the player's cup if it is less than five. These beans must be returned to the Mexican Bean Bowl. If a player does not have any beans, the play passes to the next player. If a player draws the word "Mexico," all other players shout "Ole!" Three beans must be given to each game player from the player's personal cup. If the player does not have enough beans, whichever amount is lacking should be taken from the Mexican Bean Bowl to make up the difference.

Win: After all cards are drawn, the player with the most beans is declared the winner. All help to put away the game pieces.

Variation for younger players

Game I: Play with one die. Players take turns rolling the die. Players count the numbers (up to six) in Spanish as they take beans from the Mexican Bean Bowl. A player who rolls six, shouts "Ole!" and takes six beans, he/she rolls the die again. There are no penalties in this version.

Game II: Use two dice. Players take one to ten beans from the Mexican Bean Bowl as numbers one to ten are rolled. If twelve is the amount rolled, "Ole!" is shouted by all, and 2 two beans from the player's cup must be given to each game player. If eleven is the amount rolled, all shout "Ole!" and one bean must be given from the player's cup to each game player. If a player does not have enough beans, the amount lacking should be taken from the Mexican Bean Bowl to make up the difference.

12. Obtain more information on Mexico: Consulate General of Mexico, 8 East 41st Street, New York, NY 10017 Telephone: (212) 689-0456 or Embassy of Mexico, 1911 Pennsylvania Avenue, NW, Washington, DC 20006 Telephone: (202) 728-1600.

BOOKS TO READ

Bingo Book #4 Spanish/Espanol
Helen Garvey
Foreign language games

The Boy Who Could Do Anything and Other Folk Tales
Anita Brenner
Mexican folk tales

Family Pictures
Carmen Lomas Garza
Memories of a Mexican family

Friends from the Other Side
Gloria Anzaldua
A young boy and his mother cross the Rio Grande into Texas and get help from a young Mexican girl

Legend of the Poinsettia
Tomie de Paola
When Lucinda is unable to finish her gift for the Christmas procession, a miracle occurs

Lights on the River
Jane Resh Thomas
Teresa's memories of her grandmother and Mexico

Pablo's Tree
Pat Mora
A Mexican boy's family tradition

Pablo Remembers the Day of the Dead
George Ancona
A young Mexican boy prepares for the three-day Mexican celebration

Pequenna the Burro
Jami Parkison
Tale of burros helping to build Mexico strengthens little burro who saves the day

Save My Rainforest
Monica Zak
An eight-year-old Mexican boy's efforts to save Mexico's last rainforest

Tortillas
Alvin Gordon
A Mexican shepherd boy sings a song while watching his mother making tortillas

The Witch's Face
Eric Kimmel
A Mexican tale

THE PIÑATA

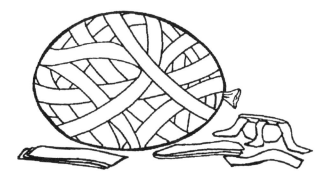

Materials
- 1/2" strips of newspaper
- wheat paste
- large balloon
- paper cups
- strong rope or wire
- scissors or knife
- poster paint/brushes
- tissue paper, feathers, crepe paper

1. Inflate and tie a large balloon.
2. Dip newspaper strips in paste and apply to balloon, approximately three layers.
3. Add paper cups and wadded news paper to balloon for legs, neck and head. Secure with newspaper strips. Let dry for several days.

4. Cut an opening in the bottom of the piñata. Pop and remove balloon.
5. Fill the cavity with candy, small toys, and other goodies. Close the opening with tape.
6. Secure a rope or wire to the top of the piñata with strips of tissue paper. Paint features on head and legs. Use beads and crepe paper for accents.

         TSD 02267-8 • *Multicultural Music*

Reboso

Tostadas

Tortillas

PEDRO

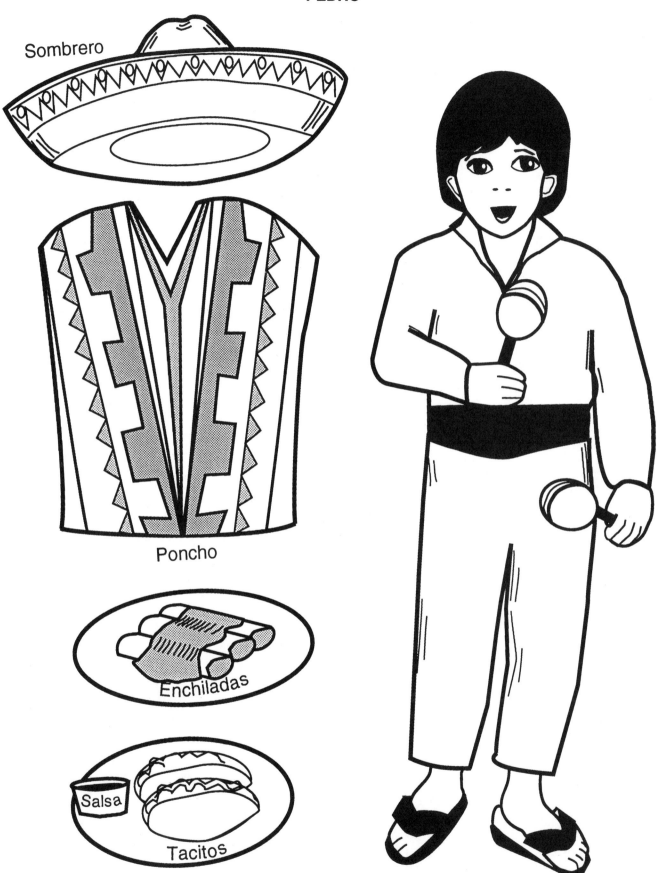

Sombrero

Poncho

Enchiladas

Salsa

Tacitos

gato

pato

gatito

perrito

patito

caballito

perro

pollito

pollo

burrito

burro

caballo

gansito

ganso

The Netherlands

The word "netherlands" means lowlands. Fifty percent of the Netherlands lies below sea level. The land below the level of the sea is nearest to the coast. A line of sand dunes, higher than the sea, prevents the North Sea from flooding the country. At times the dunes need to be strengthened or replaced. The *Nederlanders* have built numerous dikes to hold back the sea. They have drained water from the land and created farmland; this land is called a polder. There are cities built on polders. Many canals (man-made waterways) exist throughout this country. They are often higher than the level of the land through which they flow. Dikes prevent their flooding the countryside. The canals have three purposes: they are high roads for traffic, they act as drains, and they serve as boundaries for houses, fields and gardens. Bicycling is very popular; there are cycle lanes throughout the country. Dutch is the national language of the Netherlands but there are different dialects throughout the twelve provinces. The people in the province of Friesland have their own separate language, Frisian, which is recognized as an official language.

Word List

Numbers

een (ayn):		one
twee (tvay):		two
drie (dree):		three
vier (vir):		four
vijf (vyf):		five
zes (zes):		six
zeven (zay-ven):		seven
acht (ahkt):		eight
negen (nay-hen):		nine
tien (teen):		ten

Names

Anton (An-ton):	Anton
Herman (Her-man):	Herman
Pieter (Pee-ter):	Peter
Tine (Tee-ne):	Tina

Pronunciation Key

ay:	as in tr**ay**; **a**lien
y:	as in b**y**; l**ie**; s**igh**
ee:	as in l**ea**p; pr**ie**st
u:	as in d**u**st; p**u**n
a:	as in l**ah** dee d**ah**
e:	as in s**e**ven; r**e**st
i:	as in p**i**n; b**ee**r; m**i**rror
o:	as in p**o**ke; l**oa**n; r**oa**m
oo:	as in l**oo**ny; s**ou**p
j:	as in **j**am; **g**iraffe
g:	as in **g**ate; a**g**ain
s:	as in **S**anta; help**s**
z:	as in **z**oo; ea**s**y

Colors

geel (hay-le):		yellow
paarse (par-se):		purple
rode (ro-de):		red
witte (vi-te):		white

Family

grootmoeder (graowt-moo-der):	grandmother
grootvader (graowt-fa-der):	grandfather
moeder (moo-der):	mother
vader (fa-der):	father
zuster (zoos-ter):	sister

Translations

de bloemen (de-bloo-men):	flowers
fietsen (feet-sen):	to bicycle
ja (ya):	yes
Kijk naar (kyk-nar):	look at
klompen (klomp-en):	clogs
de rozen (de ro-zen):	roses
de tulpen (de to-pen):	tulips
welkom (vel-kom):	welcome

Definitions

Amsterdam: capital of the Netherlands, a leading trade center and great banking and cultural center

clogs: traditional Dutch shoes made of wood; presently worn only by a few farmers and fishermen and bought by tourists

Delft: a city in the Netherlands known for its blue and white pottery

dike: a wall or embankment built to hold back water and prevent floods

Holland: two of the twelve provinces in the Netherlands are North Holland and South Holland; they are the most populated provinces. Because of their importance historically and economically, foreigners have given the name Holland to the entire Netherlands

Kuekenhof (ke-ken-hof): famous beautiful gardens in the Netherlands

Lake Ijssel (ay-sel): a freshwater lake created when the Dutch decided to close off the Zuider Zee from the North Sea

Loosdrecht Lakes (los-dret): former peat bogs that are now inland lakes between the cities of Utrecht and Amsterdam

Madurodam (ma-doo-ro-dam): a miniature town complete with canals, railroads, stores, factories and ships that move built in a park at Madurodam, just outside The Hague; it is visited annually by thousands of people

Rembrandt: a famous Dutch artist; one of the great masters of European art

Rijksmuseum (ryks-moo-zay-um): one of the better art museums in the world

River Waal (val-ken-burg): one of the main rivers in the Netherlands known for trading; it branches off from the Rhine

Valkenburg: a town in the Netherlands in the southern province of Limburg

Wadden Zee (va-den-zee): the name given to the Zuider Zee after it was closed off from the North Sea

windmills: a machine powered by a wheel of adjustable blades or vanes that are powered by the wind; commonly seen in western Netherlands are polder mills which for years have pumped out surplus underground water that threatens to flood the polders (drained and protected pieces of ground)

The official name for the Netherlands is the "Kingdom of the Netherlands" but many foreigners call this country, Holland. The people are the Nederlanders but are known as the Dutch.

LET'S GO TO THE NETHERLANDS
(Melody: Aiken Drum)

Oh, let's go to the Netherlands
Netherlands, Netherlands
Oh, let's go to the Netherlands
There's so much I want to see.

And we'll see the dikes and windmills
The windmills, the windmills
And we'll see the dikes and windmills
In the Netherlands we'll be.

Oh, let's go to the Rijksmuseum (1)
Rijksmuseum, Rijksmuseum
Oh, let's go to the Rijksmuseum
There's so much I want to see.

And we'll see the works of Rembrandt
Of Rembrandt, Of Rembrandt
And we'll see the works of Rembrandt
In the Netherlands we'll be.

Oh, let's ride bikes to Amsterdam
Amsterdam, Amsterdam
Oh, let's ride bikes to Amsterdam
There's so much I want to see.

And we'll count the many bridges (2)
And bridges, and bridges
And we'll cross canals and bridges
In the Netherlands we'll be.

Oh, let's go to the Kuekenhof (3)
Kuekenhof, Kuekenhof
Oh, let's go to the flower fields
There's so much I want to see.

And we'll see roses and tulips
And tulips, and tulips
And we'll see roses and tulips
In the Netherlands we'll be.

Oh, let's go to Madurodam (4)
Madurodam, Madurodam
Oh, let's go to the Madurodam
There's so much I want to see.

And we'll tour the miniature village
The village, the village
And we'll tour the miniature village
In the Netherlands we'll be.

Oh, let's go to the town of Delft (5)
Town of Delft, town of Delft
Oh, let's go to the town of Delft
There's so much I want to see.

And we'll buy some clogs and pottery
Pottery, pottery
And we'll buy some clogs and pottery
In the Netherlands we'll be.

Oh, let's go to the Netherlands
Netherlands, Netherlands
Oh, let's go to the Netherlands
There's so much I want to see.

Word List: *dikes, windmills, Rijksmuseum, Rembrandt, Amsterdam, Kuekenhof, Madurodam, Delft, clogs, pottery*

Interesting Facts:
1. The Rijksmuseum with its works by Rembrandt, Vermeer, and Hals is one of the better art museums in the world. The Vincent Van Gogh Museum in Amsterdam is also very popular.

2. There are 550 bridges in Amsterdam, more than any other city in the world.

3. The Kuekenhof in Lisse is famous for its beautiful gardens. Other well-known flower fields are in the region between Haarlem and Leiden.

4. Madurodam is a historically correct reproduction of an average Dutch city and its surroundings, everything to a scale of 1:25.

5. The city of Delft is known for making glazed earthenware, usually decorated in blue on a white background.

So many of the Dutch people enjoy long-distance skating on the canals. Thousands participate in a 124-mile race, the Elfstedentocht, along frozen canals that run through eleven towns in Friesland.

WATER FUN IN HOLLAND
(Melody: John Jacob Jingleheimer Schmidt)

Holland has so many canals
Lakes and rivers, too
We'll sail on Lake Ijssel
And skate on the canal.
There are so many things for us to do
La-la-la-la-la-la-la!

Holland has so many canals
Lakes and rivers, too
We'll swim in Wadden Zee
And dive in Loosdrecht Lake.
There are so many things for us to do
La-la-la-la-la-la-la!

Holland has so many canals
Lakes and rivers, too
We'll row on River Waal
Catch herring in the Sea.
There are so many things for us to do
La-la-la-la-la-la-la!

Holland has so many canals
Lakes and rivers too
Play hockey on the ice
Leap over the canal.
There are so many things for us to do
La-la-la-la-la-la-la!

Word List: *Holland, Lake Ijssel, Wadden Zee, Loosdrecht Lake, River Waal*

Interesting Facts:
Fierljeppen (far leaping), also known as pole or canal vaulting, has become quite a sport in the Netherlands. Contestants take a running leap off a pier, grab an aluminum pole (that is stuck in the bottom of the canal and angled toward the pier), climb to the top of the pole in approximately five seconds, and push off into a sand pit. Ljeppers, mostly men, range in age from under ten to over sixty.

Bicycling is a primary means of transportation in Holland. As a young girl in the Netherlands, Marian Mathes of Hamburg, Michigan, recalls the wind, rain and snow on her face as she rode her bike to school everyday.

A-FIETSEN WE WILL GO or A-BIKING WE WILL GO
(Melody: A-Hunting We Will Go)

Oh, a-fietsen we will go*
A-fietsen we will go
Through rain and snow, the wind will blow
A-fietsen we will go.

Oh, I'll bike my way to school
I'll bike my way to school
I'll get all wet but what the heck
I'll bike my way to school.

Oh, I'll bike to Valkenburg
I'll bike to Valkenburg
I'll ride to town; I'll shop around
I'll bike to Valkenburg.

Oh, a-fietsen we will go*
A-fietsen we will go
Through rain and snow, the wind will blow
A-fietsen we will go.

Oh, I'll bike to the parade
I'll bike to the parade
I'll get so cold but still I'll go
I'll bike to the parade.

Oh, I'll win a biking race
I'll win a biking race
I'll get a prize; a nice surprise
I'll win a biking race.

Oh, a-fietsen we will go*
A-fietsen we will go
Through rain and snow, the wind will blow
A-fietsen we will go

Word List: *Valkenburg, fietsen*

*The alternative to this refrain is:
Oh, a-biking we will go
A-biking we will go
Through rain and snow, the wind will blow
A-biking we will go.

WELKOM
(Melody: My Hand On My Head)

Knock knock on the door
Who could it be?
It is my grandmother,
That's who I see
Grootmoeder, grootmoeder
Won't you please come in?
Tell me just how have you been?
Ja! Ja!

Knock knock on the door
Who could it be?
It is my grandfather
That's who I see
Grootvader, grootvader
Won't you please come in?
Tell me just how have you been?
Ja! Ja!

Knock knock on the door
Who could it be?
It is my mother, yes
That's who I see
Moeder, oh, moeder, now
Won't you please come in?
Tell me just how have you been?
Ja! Ja!

Knock knock on the door
Who could it be?
It is my father, yes
That's who I see
Vader, oh, vader, now
Won't you please come in?
Tell me just how have you been?
Ja! Ja!

Knock knock on the door
Who could it be?
It is my sister, yes
That's who I see
Zuster, oh, zuster, now
Won't you please come in?
Tell me just how have you been?
Ja! Ja!

Knock knock on the door
Who could it be?
These are my friends here, yes
That's who I see
Pieter and Anton and
Tine and Herman, now
Won't you please come in?
Tell me just how have you been?
Ja! Ja!

> **Word List:** *Welkom, grootmoeder, ja, grootvader, moeder, vader, zuster, Pieter, Anton, Tine, Herman*

DUTCH NUMBERS
(Melody: Love Somebody)

One, two, three is een, twee, drie
Four, five, six is vier, vijf, zes
Seven, eight is zeven, acht
Nine and ten in Dutch are negen, tien.

Een, twee, drie is one, two, three
Vier, vijf, zes is four, five, six
Zeven, acht is seven, eight
Negen, tien is Dutch for nine and ten.

> **Word List:** *een, twee, drie, vier, vijf, zes, zeven, acht, negen, tien*

Dutch flower bulbs are famous all over the world. Several thousand kinds of tulips are grown, plus plentiful hyacinths, daffodils, and crocuses. The leading flowers cultivated are roses, chrysanthemums, and carnations.

LOOK AT THE FLOWERS
(Melody: Shortnin' Bread)

Kjik naar de bloemen; see over there
Look at all the flowers growing everywhere!
I see zes rode bloemen there
There are six red flowers growing in the square
I see zes rode bloemen—they're growing, growing
I see six red flowers now over there
I see zes rode bloemen—they're growing, growing
I see six red flowers now over there.

Kjik naar de tulpen; see over there
Look at all the tulips growing everywhere!
I see zes rode tulpen there
There are six red tulips growing in the square
I see zes rode tulpen—they're growing, growing
I see six red tulips now over there
I see zes rode tulpen—they're growing, growing
I see six red tulips now over there.

Kjik naar de rozen; see over there
Look at all the flowers growing everywhere!
I see zes rode rozen there
There are six red roses growing in the square
I see zes rode rozen—they're growing, growing
I see six red roses now over there
I see zes rode rozen- they're growing, growing
I see six red roses now over there.

> **Word List:** *Kjik naar, de bloemen, zes, rode, bloemen, tulpen, rozen*

Other choices:
tien witte bloemen (tulpen, rozen): ten white flowers (tulips, roses)
vijf gele bloemen (tulpen, rozen): five yellow flowers (tulips, roses)
vier paarse bloemen (tulpen): four purple flowers (tulips)

Klompen were originally worn to protect Dutch feet from getting wet. Today in the Netherlands, only a few farmers, gardeners, and fishermen wear these wooden shoes. At festive activities, dancers in traditional Dutch clothing and wooden shoes stomp in rhythm for entertainment and pleasure.

KLOMPEN DANCE
(Melody: Pony Boy)

Stomp your feet; stomp your feet	*(stomp RIGHT, left, right; left, right, left)*
Come with me; dance in the street	*(clap hands)*
Lift one shoe; stomp it thrice	*(lift RIGHT foot; stomp three times starting on "stomp")*
Wooden shoes are nice	*(clap hands)*
Een, twee, drie; een, twee, drie	*(stomp LEFT, right; left, right, left, right)*
Put your arm in mine	*(lock arms with a partner)*
Turn around; turn around	*(slowly turn around together)*
Turn around, stop!	*(turn around and stop)*
It's klompen time!	*(stomp LEFT, right, left, right)*
Stomp your feet; stomp your feet	*(stomp LEFT, right, left, right, left, right)*
Come with me; dance in the street	*(clap hands)*
Lift one shoe; stomp it thrice	*(lift LEFT foot; stomp three times starting on "stomp")*
Wooden shoes are nice.	*(clap hands)*
Een, twee, drie; een, twee, drie	*(stomp RIGHT, left, right; left, right, left)*
Put your arm in mine	*(lock arms with a partner)*
Turn around; turn around	*(slowly turn around together)*
Turn around, stop!	*(turn around and stop)*
It's klompen time!	*(stomp RIGHT, left, right, left)*

> **Word List:** *klompen, een, twee, drie*

THE HOLE IN THE DIKE
(Verse Melody: Pretty Little Dutch Girl – Refrain Melody: Playmate)

This song is based on a famous story from "Hans Brinker," also known as "The Silver Skates." Although the story is fiction, people around the world go to The Netherlands looking for the location of this well-known scene. The Dutch people have erected a statue of the little boy in this story to signify their devotion and dedication to keeping their country safe from the sea.

There was a boy named Peter
Who lived so long ago
He loved his country very much
He is a great hero.

(refrain)
Oh, little Peter, how very brave you are
You stayed awake all night, your finger in the dike
You love your country—the town and people too
You saved them from a flood; we're proud of you!

Now Peter went to visit
A friend across the way
He stayed so long; it was so dark
The shortcut he would take.

Oh, little Peter, how very brave you are
You stayed awake all night, your finger in the dike
You love your country—the town and people, too
You saved them from a flood; we're proud of you!

He heard some water trickling
'Twas coming from the dike
He screamed for help; his cry rang out
But no one came that night.

Oh, little Peter, how very brave you are
You stayed awake all night, your finger in the dike
You love your country—the town and people, too
You saved them from a flood; we're proud of you!

The milkman came next morning
He thought he heard a shout
He ran through town; woke people up
To help that poor boy out.

Oh, little Peter, how very brave you are
You stayed awake all night, your finger in the dike
You love your country—the town and people, too
You saved them from a flood; we're proud of you!

The people came to help him
He was so wet and cold
They picked him up and gave a cheer,
"Hurray for our hero!"

Oh, little Peter, how very brave you are
You stayed awake all night, your finger in the dike
You love your country—the town and people, too
You saved them from a flood; we're proud of you!

ALLE EENDJES ZWEMMEN IN HET WATER
(All the Ducks are Swimming in the Water)

Al- le eend-jes zwem- men in het wa- ter, fal - de- ral- de- rie- re, fal - de- ral- de- rie- re,

al- le eend- jes zwem- men in het wa- ter, fal, fal, fal - de- ral- de ra.

All the ducks are swimming in the water
Fal-de-ral-de-rie-re, fal-de-ral-de-rie-re,
All the ducks are swimming in the water
Fal-fal fal-de-ral-de-ra

HOP, HOP, HOP, PAARDJE IN GALOP
(Hop, Hop, Hop Galloping Horse)

Hop, hop, hop, paar- dje in ga - lop! O - ver hek en slo- ten he- nen,

maar voor- zich- tig, breek geen be- nen. Hop, hop, hop! Paar- dje in ga - lop.

Hop, hop, hop galloping horse
Over fence; across the water
But take care and break no legs now
Hop, hop, hop galloping horse

ZEG MOEDER, WAAR IS JAN?
(Say Mother, Where is John?)

Zeg moe- der, waar is Jan? Daar gin - der, daar gin - der. Zeg

moe- der, waar is Jan? Daar gin - der komt hij an.

Say mother, where is John?	Where has he been?	What did he have there?
Over there, over there	At auntie's, at auntie's	A cookie, a cookie
Say mother, where is John?	Where has he been?	What did he have there?
Over there he comes	At auntie's, at her party.	A cookie with a hole!

   TSD 02267-8 • *Multicultural Music*

Saucijzebroodjes (so-say-ze-bro-ges) (sausage sandwiches)
Ingredients:
2 1/2 cups flour, 2 tsp. baking powder, 1 tsp. salt, 1/2 cup shortening, 1 egg, 1/2 cup milk or more,
1 lb. steak and 1 lb. veal steak ground together
1. Mix and sift dry ingredients.
2. Cut in shortening as for pie crust.
3. Beat egg; add milk and dry ingredients; more milk may be needed to make a soft dough of proper consistency to roll out to 1/2 inch thickness.
4. Season the meat (salt, pepper, nutmeg); make small rolls about three inches long and one inch in thickness.
5. Cover each roll with the pastry. Bake in hot oven for 30 minutes.

Stamppot (stam-pot) (vegetable or vegetable/meat dish)
Ingredients:
Mashed potatoes, cooked carrots
1. Cook carrots; cook potatoes and mash with a small amount of liquid.
2. Mix together; season to taste with salt and pepper (nutmeg, optional).
3. Add meat or cheese (if desired, add cooked bacon, sausage, or small cubes of cheese).

Speculaatjes (spay-koo-la-jes) (spiced cookies)
Ingredients:
1 cup butter, 4 tsp. cinnamon, 1 cup shortening, 1/2 tsp. nutmeg, 2 cups brown sugar, 1/2 tsp. cloves, 1/2 cup sour cream, 4 1/2 cups sifted flour, 1/2 tsp. baking soda, 1/2 cup chopped almonds
1. Cream the butter, shortening, and sugar.
2. Add sour cream alternately with sifted dry ingredients.
3. Stir in almonds.
4. Knead the dough into rolls; wrap in waxed paper; chill overnight.
5. Roll dough very thin and cut into shapes.
6. Bake at 375° for 10 to 15 minutes.

Banket Staven (ban-ket stav-en) (Clara Walters' almond rolls)
Ingredients:
1/2 cup butter, 3 cups sifted flour, 1/2 cup ice water, 2 Tbsp. vinegar, 1 1/4 lbs. almond paste, 1 1/2 cups sugar, 2 eggs (slightly beaten).
1. Cut butter into flour as for pastry; add water and vinegar mixing well. Chill thoroughly.
2. Divide dough into four portions. Roll each portion into a rectangle 4" x 12."
3. Crumble almond paste, add 1 1/2 cups sugar. Blend with pastry blender.
4. Add eggs, chill thoroughly.
5. Shape almond paste mixture into four rolls about eleven inches long. Shaping rolls on lightly floured cloth makes them easier to handle.
6. Place a roll of almond paste on a pastry rectangle. Brush on long edge with water.
7. Roll a pastry around filling, rolling toward wet edge. Pinch ends together.
8. Place rolls on ungreased cookie sheets with seam side down. Brush with mixture of egg and milk.
9. Prick with fork.
10. Bake at 400° for 15 minutes, then 320° for 20 minutes.

Pepermuntkussentjes (pay-per-munt-ke-sent-yes) (after dinner mints)
Ingredients:
1/4 lb. of confectionery sugar, 1 or 2 drops of peppermint oil, 1/2 beaten egg white
1. Sift sugar; continue stirring while adding egg white and oil until you have a stiff, smooth paste.
2. Roll into long rolls (pencil thickness) on a board sprinkled with confectionery sugar. Cut these long strips with scissors into small square pieces. Let stiffen in a cool place.

Activities

1. Although most windmills are no longer in use, their sight is a pleasure to visitors from all over the world. In the past, the sails of the windmills were set to let others know if the mill was working or not, or to announce a birth, death, or special occasion. Children can make a windmill and set sails to send messages. Each student will need a one-quart milk carton, paper to cover the milk carton, four plastic drinking straws, one round unsharpened pencil with eraser, and one push pin.

   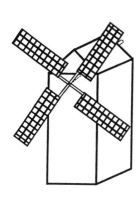

   Instructions:
   1. Milk cartons must be rinsed out and air-dried thoroughly.
   2. Cover cartons with adhesive paper.
   3. Make one small hole in the front and one in the back of the milk carton through which to slide the pencil.
   4. Cross two plastic straws and staple together in the center.
   5. Make the blades by cutting four rectangles 3 1/2" by 1 1/2" from colored construction paper; make crossbars by drawing lines as shown in the illustration; staple sails to the ends of the straws.
   6. Stick the pin through the center of the straws and into the eraser of the pencil.
   7. Insert the pencil through the front and out the back holes in the milk carton.

   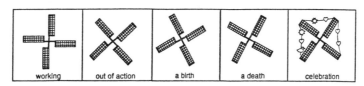

2. Students can sing and dance the *Klompen Dance* song (page 134). They can also sing the song while manipulating their own Klompen puppets (marionettes). Have the children create their own puppets. Attach arms and legs with brads.

3. The children will have fun making Dutch candy. The pepermuntkussentjes (recipe on page 136) are to be rolled and cut into pieces.

4. Have students plant tulip bulbs in pots for a spring Tulip Festival celebration.

5. Celebrate Tulip Festival Time when the children's tulips are in bloom. Have children make paper tulips to decorate the room. Ask for items from Holland for display. Offer parents the Dutch recipes in the recipe section and ask for volunteers to cook Dutch food. Children can sing the songs they have learned and dance the Klompen Dance.

6. Celebrate Orange Day, Koninginnedag, the birthday of Queen Julianna of the House of Orange on April 30th. It is a holiday filled with parades, games, song, and dance. The ancestors of the royal family came from Orange, France. Queen Julianna picks two Dutch cities to visit each year with her family. The children in the town and nearby villages gather to sing old Dutch songs, the national anthem and take part in various activities. Include some of these activities in your celebration of Orange Day. Play your own version of the games. Add other orange activities such as orange decorations, foods, drinks, and projects using orange paint, paper, and craft material.
   - **Ringsteken** - a ring toss game. Two people sit on a cart drawn by a horse. There is a gate made of wood with a pail of water on the top. If the participants are not successful in tossing a ring through a larger ring hanging at the top of the gate, a string is pulled and the pail of water empties on their heads.
   - **Zaklopen** - a potato sack race with big bags of burlap sacks
   - **Sjoelen** - a Dutch game played by sliding disks into holes in a big wooden board

7. Read the book, *The Hole in the Dike* (listed in the book section). Then teach the children the song *"The Hole in the Dike"* on page 134.

8. For more information about the Netherlands, write or call: Consulate General of the Netherlands, One Rockefeller Plaza, 11th Floor, New York, NY 10020, Telephone (212) 246-1429 or Embassy of the Netherlands, 4200 Linnean Avenue, NW, Washington, DC 20008, Telephone (202) 244-5300.

BOOKS TO READ

Anna is Still Here
I. Vos
Story of a thirteen year old survivor of Nazi-occupied Holland

Anne Frank
Brown
Autobiography of a thirteen-year-old Jewish girl hiding from the Nazis

Father, May I Come?
P. Spier
Sietze Hemmes sets in motion the rescue of a floundering ship off the Dutch coast

The First Book of the Netherlands
Angelo Cohn
The people, land, and culture by the author who lived several years with a family in the Netherlands

The First Tulips in Holland
P. Krasilovsky
Fictionalized account of how a Dutch merchant brought tulip bulbs from Persia to Holland

The Hole in the Dike
Retold by Norma Green
illustrated by Eric Carle
The famous legend of the boy who saved his country

Hurrah for a Dutch Birthday
Antonia Ridge and Mies Bonhuge
Wilhelmina called Mina and her birthday verlanglijst (wish list)

Jerry Lives in Holland
David Hampton
Black and white photographs depict a boy's family life

The Legend of New Amsterdam
Peter Spier
The story of the beginning of the city and its people

Looking At Holland
A. Loman
Sixty-three pages of photographs

The Netherlands
D. Cumming
Twelve children from all over the Netherlands describe geography, weather, industry, and culture

Rembrandt
Mike Venezia
A simple book for children about the famous Dutch painter

We Live in the Netherlands
Preben Kristensn and Frona Cameron
Accounts of people and their occupations in the Netherlands

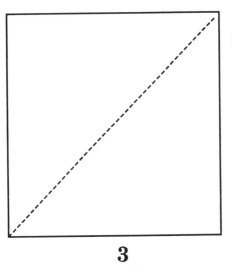

DUTCH HAT

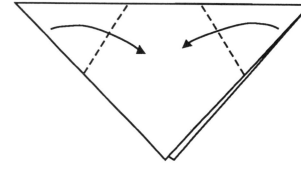

3

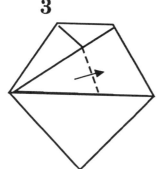

4
Front

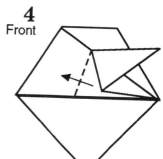

5
Front

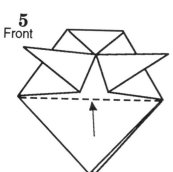

6
Back

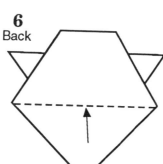

7
Front

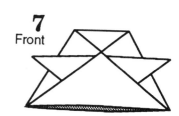

Directions for the Klompen Dancers

Patterns found on pages 140-141.

1. Glue copies of the Dutch boy and girl onto sturdy paper or posterboard.
2. Color and cut out the various parts.
3. Connect all the body parts together with brads.
4. Prick a tiny hole into the top of each arm piece; tie a small length of thread between the two holes as illustrated in the diagram.
5. Follow the same procedure in step four on the leg pieces.
6. Connect all the threads by tying one long thread in the center of each of the smaller threads as illustrated. The long thread must hang down below the puppet. When it is pulled, the arms and legs will kick out.
7. Glue the cork on the back of the puppet's head. Push the dowel rod into the cork.
8. Hold the stick in one hand; pull the long thread with the other hand.

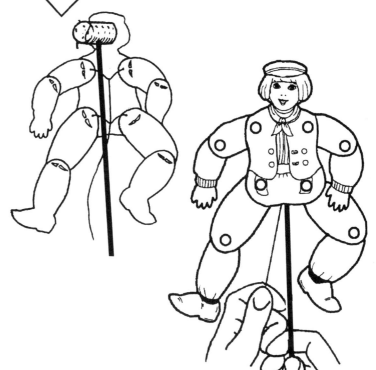

　　　139　　　TSD 02267-8 • *Multicultural Music*

KLOMPEN BOY DANCER PATTERN

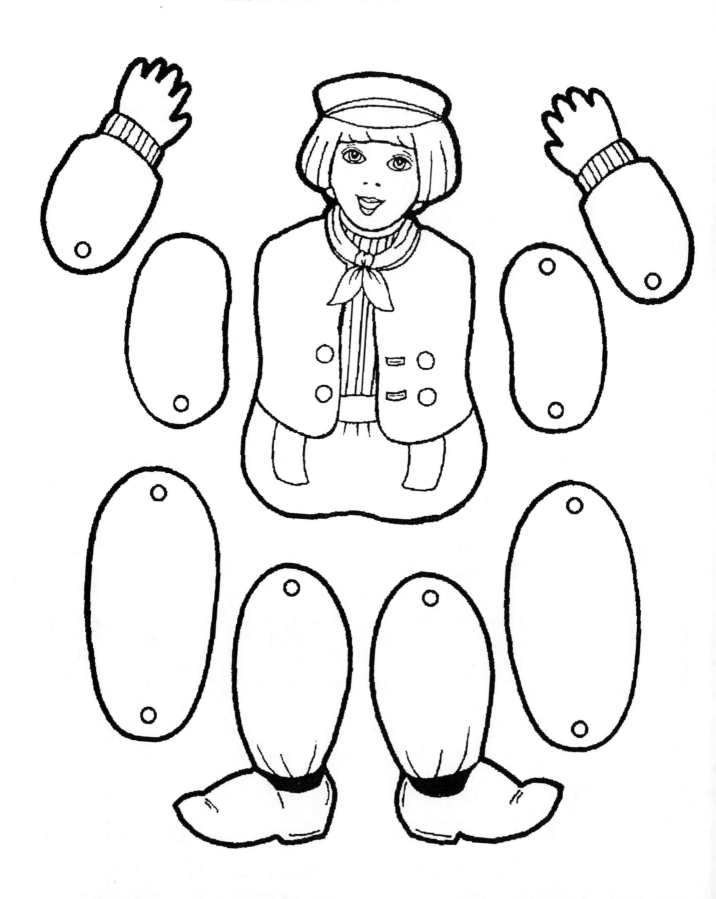

KLOMPEN GIRL DANCER PATTERN

Poland

Although there are rolling hills in parts of Poland and mountains in the south, most of Poland is flat. This explains the meaning of its name. It comes from the Polish word "pola" which means fields or plains. At one time, Poland was a dominant power in Eastern Europe. Through the centuries, foreign powers have divided Poland and twice it even ceased to exist. Today it is emerging as a liberal democracy. The three major cities in Poland are Warsaw, Kraków, and Gdańsk. Warsaw, the capital of Poland, was almost completely destroyed in World War II and has been totally rebuilt. Kraków, the ancient royal capital, has many historical sites such as the castle, coronation chapel, and burial chambers of the Polish kings. Gdańsk is the largest port on the Baltic sea. The Polish people are known to be hard-working, hospitable and persevering. Famous and distinguished Poles are: Copernicus, astronomer and mathematician; Marie Curie, physicist and chemist; Frédéric Chopin, composer and celebrated pianist; Ignace Jan Paderewski, pianist, composer and statesman; Henryk Sienkiewicz, Nobel Prize winner and historical novelist (*Quo Vadis?*); Karol Wojtyla, former Archbishop of Kracow, now John Paul II, Pope of the Roman Catholic Church; and Lech Walesa, leader of the Solidarity movement who was elected president of Poland in 1990.

Word List for Poland

Numbers

jeden (ye-den)	one
dwa (de-va)	two
trzy (che)	three
cztery (shte-re)	four
pieć (eeinch)	five
sieść (shesh)	six
siedem (she-dem)	seven
osiem (osh-em)	eight
dziewięć (je-vee-aynsh)	nine
dziesięć (je-shaynsh)	ten

Pronunciation Key

ay: as in tr**ay**; **a**lien
y: as in b**y**; **lie**; s**igh**
ee: as in l**ea**p; pr**ie**st
u: as in d**u**st; p**u**n
a: as in l**a**h dee dah
e: as in s**e**ven; r**e**st
i: as in p**i**n; b**ee**r; m**i**rror
o: as in p**o**ke; l**oa**n; r**oa**m
oo: as in l**oo**ny; s**ou**p
j: as in **j**am; **g**iraffe
g: as in **g**ate; a**g**ain
s: as in **S**anta; help**s**
z: as in **z**oo; ea**s**y

Food

chrusciki (roos-chee-kee): a favorite dessert, sometimes called angel wings, sweet crisps or crullers
golabki (go-wum-kee): stuffed cabbage
kapusta (ka-poos-ta): cabbage, a favorite dish when cooked with onions and lima beans or fried with onions
kielbasa (ki-bas-a): sausage
pączki (punch-kee): Polish-style jelly doughnuts; a favorite treat on Shrove Tuesday, Pączki Day
pierogi (pee-er-o-gee): dumplings filled with mashed potatoes, cooked cabbage, fried onions, and dry cheese; served as an entree or filled with sweet cheese, apples, cherries or blueberries and served as a dessert

Dances

krakowiak (kra-ko-vee-ak): a very popular folk dance from the Krakow region
mazurek (mu-zur ek): a lively dance from the Mazovia (Marzowsza) region in Poland
oberek (o-ber-ek): a Polish folk dance in 3/8 tempo
polka (pol-ka): a lively dance consisting of a pattern of three steps and a skip or hop
polonaise (po-lo-nez): a slow, stately dance of Polish origin, in three-quarter time; it is mainly a promenade of couples
walczek (val-chek): the waltz, a favorite dance with many Polish village people before World War II

Folk Art

kraszanki (kra-shan-kee): boiled eggs dyed in plant materials such as onion skins, and beet leaves

malowanki (ma-lo-van-kee): eggs that have been hand-painted

nalepianki (na-li-peean-kee): blown-out eggs with designs made of paper, straw, or fabric glued on the solid-color dyed shell

pisanki (pee-san-kee): eggs dyed in various colors after wax designs have been applied between each dye

Translations

babcia (bab-cha): grandmother

Ciocia Rózia (Cha-cha Rooj-a): Aunt Rose

Dobranoc (do-bra-nots): good night

dziadek (ja-dek): grandfather

Dziękuję (jayn-koo-ye): thank you

Dzień Dobry (jayn do-bray): good day

krakowianki (kra-ko-vee-an-kee): girls in traditional, festive costumes who dance the krakowiak

Matka i Ojciec (mat-ka ee oy-chets): Mother and Father

Definitions

amber: a hard yellow or yellowish-brown gum, the resin of fossil pine trees; amber is translucent and easily polished and is used for jewelry

Chopin: famous composer and pianist who wrote nocturnes, mazurkas, and polonaises evoking the Polish national character

Łazienki Palace (waj-en-kee): a charming palace on the water in the Royal Łazienki Park in Warsaw, also known as Poniatowski Palace

Tatry Mountains (tat-re): a range of mountains in southern Poland, snow-covered from December through March

Wawel Castle (va-vel): the royal residence of former Polish kings located near Kraków (Cracow in English)

*This song is dedicated
to my grandparents who came from Poland.*

A VISIT TO POLAND
*(Melodies: Refrain—Jim Crack Corn
Verse—Going To Kentucky)*

Oh, Poland's where I want to go
Poland's where I want to go
Poland's where I want to go
I'll take you there with me!

My dziadek came from Poland
My babcia, she did too
Someday I'd like to travel
And visit there with you
We'll call on Ciocia Rózia
She'll cook great food to eat
Kapusta and kielbasa
Chrusciki for a treat.

Oh, Poland's where I want to go
Poland's where I want to go
Poland's where I want to go
I'll take you there with me!

We'll drive up to Wieliczka
See carvings in the mines
Then climb the Tatry Mountains
To see what we can find
We'll look for krakowianki
At festivals and fairs
Drive to Wawel Castle
To see the treasures there.

Oh, Poland's where I want to go
Poland's where I want to go
Poland's where I want to go
I'll take you there with me!

We'll tour Łazienki Palace
The gardens we must see
We'll hear them playing Chopin
Let's go to symphonies
We'll buy some amber earrings
Boxes carved from wood
Souvenirs of Poland
Our trip will be so good!

Oh, Poland's where I want to go
Poland's where I want to go
Poland's where I want to go
I'll take you there with me!

Word List: *dziadek, babcia, Ciocia Rózia,
kapusta, kielbasa, chrusciki, Wieliczka,
Tatry Mountains, krakowianki, Wawel Castle,
Łazienki Palace, Chopin, amber*

MATKA I OJCIEC
*(Melody: Boom, Boom,
Ain't It Great To Be Crazy?)*

Dzień Dobry in Polish is "Good Day"
Dzień Dobry in Polish is "Good Day"
Matka i Ojciec is Mother and Dad
Dzień Dobry in Polish is "Good Day."

Dziękuję in Polish is "Thank You"
Dziękuję in Polish is "Thank You"
Matka i Ojciec is Mother and Dad
Dziękuję in Polish is "Thank You."

Dobranoc in Polish is "Good night"
Dobranoc in Polish is "Good night"
Matka i Ojciec is "Mother and Dad"
Dobranoc in Polish is "Good night."

Word List: *Dzień dobry, Matka i Ojciec,
dziękuję, dobranoc*

ONE IS JEDEN
(Melody: Are You Sleeping?)

One is jeden; one is jeden
Two is dwa; two is dwa
Number three is trzy
Number three is trzy
One, two, three
Jeden, dwa, trzy.

Four is cztery; four is cztery
Five is pięć; five is pięć
Number six is sieść
Number six is sieść
Four, five, six; cztery, pięć, sieść.

Seven is siedem; seven is siedem
Eight is osiem; eight is osiem
Number nine is dziewięć
Number nine is dziewięć
Seven, eight, nine
Siedem, osiem, dziewięć.

Ten is dziesięć; ten is dziesięć
One, two, three; jeden, dwa, trzy
Four, five, six and seven;
cztery, pięć, sieść, siedem
Eight, nine, ten;
osiem, dziewięć, dziesięć.

Word List: *jeden, dwa, trzy, cztery, pięć, sieść,
siedem, osiem, dziewięć, dziesięć*

The decoration of eggs has been a part of Polish history for thousands of years. Eggs with painted and scratched designs have been discovered dating back to prehistoric times. Each region of Poland has its own special techniques for the decoration of eggs as well as its very own patterns for pisanki and malowanki.

PISANKI
(Melody: A-Tisket, A-Tisket)

Pisanki, pisanki
Come decorate pisanki
We'll color eggs and make designs
Yes, we will have a happy time.

Kraszanki, kraszanki
Now come and dye kraszanki
We'll boil eggs with onion skins
And give them to our friends and kin.

Malowanki, malowanki
Come paint some malowanki
We'll paint some eggs; they're made of wood
And give to them to our neighborhood.

Nalepianki, nalepianki
Come trim some nalepianki
With straw and paper and some glue
Such pretty eggs for me and you.

Word List: *pisanki, kraszanki, malowanki, nalepianki*

pisanki - two techniques are employed for creating pisanki: (1) designs on melted wax applied with a stylus and placed into dyes of two or more colors and (2) designs scratched into an egg shell after the egg has been dyed a single color

kraszanki - hard-boiled eggs colored in vegetable dyes; onion skins are used throughout Poland; other plant materials were used from region to region such as crocus petals, beets, plums, grass, moss, spinach, sunflower seeds, blackberries, coffee, and walnut shells

malowanki - hollow or wooden eggs brush-painted with colorful designs copied from embroidery stitches; most commonly found in central and southern Poland

nalepianki - hollow eggs decorated with brightly colored paper, straw, or scraps of fabric; different material is used for this ornamentation in the various regions of Poland depending on what plant life can be found locally

---

Although western-style music and clothing are preferred to those of past generations, cultural centers strive to keep Polish heritage alive by encouraging folk dancing in traditional costumes at festivals and celebrations. The villagers of southern Poland include a folk dance in their festivities. It is the polka which became a very popular Polish-American dance.

POLISH DANCES
(Melody: Reuben, Rachel)

(girls sing)
Stasiu*, Stasiu, hurry, hurry
It is almost time to go
We'll be dancing the krakowiak
It's the only dance I know.
> *(boys sing)*
> Zosia*, Zosia, hurry, hurry
> It is almost time to go
> We'll be dancing the mazurek
> It's the only dance I know.

(girls sing)
Stasiu, Stasiu, hurry, hurry
It is almost time to go
We'll be learning the oberek
We'll just have to do it slow.
> *(boys sing)*
> Zosia, Zosia, hurry, hurry
> It is almost time to go
> We can learn to do the walczek
> It's the dance that they do slow.

Pronunciation on page 147

Word List: *Stasiu, krakowiak, Zosia, mazurek, oberek, walczek*

THE POLKA
(Melody: Throw It Out the Window)

The polka, the polka
I love to dance the polka
Fast, slow - slow, fast
What fun to dance the polka!

Mary loved to polka so
She asked John to the dance
They twirled around and he fell down
And tore his brand new pants.

The polka, the polka
I love to dance the polka
Fast, slow - slow, fast
What fun to dance the polka!

The polka was Joe's favorite dance
He'd dance the whole night through
The next day teacher yelled at him
He fell asleep in school.

The polka, the polka
I love to dance the polka
Fast, slow - slow, fast
What fun to dance the polka!

Polish home-cooking has become well loved in restaurants and homes throughout the world. Four favorite foods are the Polish sausage, stuffed cabbage, filled dumplings, and jelly doughnuts.

HE ATE TEN FAT KIELBASA
(Melody: Band of Angels)

He ate one; He ate two
He ate three fat kielbasa
He ate four; He ate five
He ate six fat kielbasa
He ate seven; He ate eight
He ate nine fat kielbasa
Ten fat kielbasa now are gone!

Stasiu ate them all
He ate ten kielbasa
Ten kielbasa
Ten kielbasa
Stasiu ate them all
He ate ten kielbasa
Now he wants some more!
   Spoken: ***Give him twenty!***

She ate one; She ate two
She ate three fried pierogi
She ate four; She ate five
She ate six fried pierogi
She ate seven; She ate eight
She ate nine fried pierogi
Ten fried pierogi now are gone!

Stefka ate them all
She ate ten pierogi
Ten pierogi
Ten pierogi
Stefka ate them all
She ate ten pierogi
Now she wants some more!
   Spoken: ***Give her thirty!***

He ate one; He ate two
He ate three big gołabki
He ate four; He ate five
He ate six big gołabki
He ate seven; He ate eight
He ate nine big gołabki
Ten big gołabki now are gone!
Edek ate them all

He ate ten gołabki
Ten gołabki
Ten gołabki
Edek ate them all
He ate ten gołabki
Now he wants some more!
   Spoken: ***Give him forty!***

She ate one; She ate two
She ate three sugar pączki
She ate four; She ate five
She ate six sugar pączki
She ate seven; She ate eight
She ate nine sugar pączki
Ten sugar pączki now are gone!

Józia ate them all
She ate ten sugar pączki
Ten sugar pączki
Ten sugar pączki
Jósia ate them all
She ate ten sugar pączki
Now she wants some more!
   Spoken: ***Give her fifty!***

Word List: *kielbasa, Stasiu*, pierogi, Stefka*, gołabki, Edek*, pączki, Jósia**

---

* Polish Names

Stasiu (sta-shoo):	Stanley
Stefka (stef-ka):	Stephanie
Edek (ed-ek):	Eddie
Jósia (yuj-a):	Josephine
Julek (yu-lek):	Julius
Jósef (yu-zef):	Joseph
Macku (mach-koo):	Matthew
Marysia (mar-i-sha):	Mary
Janek (ya-nek):	John
Jancia (yan-cha):	Jeanette
Zosia (zo-sha):	Sophie

MARYSIU, MARYSIU

This Polish song is fun to sing! It is sung alternately by Mary and Matthew (or the boys and the girls) with the entire class singing the group parts. It is reminiscent of the American song "There's A Hole In A Bucket" with dialogue between "dear Henry" and "dear Liza."

MARYSIU
(adapted)

Matthew:	Marysiu, Marysiu Gotuj pierogi	Mary dear, Mary dear Cook some pierogi
Mary:	O mój Maćku drogi My nie mamy makę.	Oh my dearest Matthew We don't have any flour.
Group:	Więc Maciek do miasta Po makę do ciasta	So Matthew went to town To fetch flour by sundown!
Matthew:	Marysiu, Marysiu Gotuj pierogi	Mary dear, Mary dear Cook some pierogi
Mary:	O mój Maćku drogi My nie mamy sera.	Oh my dearest Matthew We don't have any dry cheese.
Group:	Więc Maciek do miasta Po serek do ciasta	So Matthew went to town To fetch cheese by sundown!
Matthew:	Marysiu, Marysiu Gotuj pierogi	Mary dear, Mary dear Cook some pierogi
Mary:	O mój Maćku drogi My nie mamy wody	Oh my dearest Matthew We don't have any water
Group:	Więc Maciek do studni Pompuje, aź dudni	Then Matthew, so they tell Brought water from the well
Matthew:	Marysiu, Marysiu Gotuj pierogi	Mary dear, Mary dear Cook some pierogi
Mary:	O mój Maćku drogi Bo ja nie umie	Oh my dearest Matthew I just don't know how!
Group:	Więc Maciek do miasta Po ksiąźke do ciasta	So Matthew went to town For a book, by sundown!
Matthew:	*(very loudly, as he gives Mary the cookbook)* Marysiu, Marysiu Gotuj pierogi!!!	*(very loudly, as he gives Mary the cookbook)* Mary dear, Mary dear Now, cook that pierogi!!!

MIAŁA BABA KOGUTA
(Once There Was A Baba)

150

PONIEDZIAŁEK RANO

On a Mon-day morn - ing, sun-ny Mon-day morn - ing,

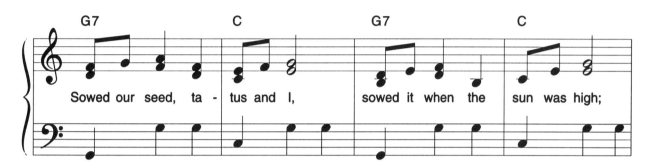

Sowed our seed, ta - tus and I, sowed it when the sun was high;

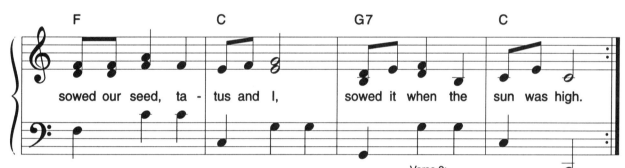

sowed our seed, ta - tus and I, sowed it when the sun was high.

Verse 2:
On a Tuesday morning, sunny Tuesday morning,
Mowed our hay, Tatus and I,
Mowed it when the sun was high...

Verse 3:
On a Wednesday morning ...
Dried our hay, Tatus and I ...

W PONIEDZIAŁEK RANO
Melody: On a Monday Morning)
(Polish Haying Song)

Verse 1:
W poniedziałek rano kosił ojciec siano,
Kosił ojciec, kosił ja, Kosiliśmy obydwa
Kosił ojciec, kosił ja,
Kosiliśmy obydwa.

Verse 2:
A we wtorek rano, grabił ojciec siano,
Grabił ojciec, grabil ja,
Grabiliśmy obydwa.

Verse 3:
A we środe rano, suszył ojciec siano,
Suszył ojciec, suszył ja,
Suszyliśmy obydwa.

Verse 4:
A we czwartek rano, zwoził ojciec siano,
Zwoził ojciec, zwoził ja,
Zwoziliśmy obydwa.

Verse 5:
A zaś w piatek rano, sprzedał ojciec siano,
Sprzedał ojciec, sprzedał ja,
Sprzedaliśmy obydwa.

Verse 6:
A w sobote rano przepił ojciec siano,
Przepił ojciec, przepil ja,
Przepiliśmy obydwa.

Verse 7:
A w niedziele ź rana, juz nie było siana,
Płakał ojciec, płakał ja
Płakaliśmy obydwa.

Verse 4:
On a Thursday morning ...
Raked our hay Tatus and I ...

Verse 5:
On a a Friday morning ...
Hauled our hay, Tatus and I ...
Hauled it until the dusk was nigh...

Verse 6:
On a Saturday morning, sunny noon and evening,
Sold our hay, Tatus and I...
Sold it when the night was nigh...

Verse 7:
On a Sunday morning, bright and sunny morning,
Bowed our heads, Tatus and I ...
Thanked the Lord who dwells on high ...

                   TSD 02267-8 • *Multicultural Music*

STO LAT
(One Hundred Years)

Pierogi with Cabbage

Ingredients:
1 1/2 lbs. cabbage (boiled), 1/2 lb. dry cottage cheese, 1 onion (chopped), 1 1/2 Tbsp. butter, salt and pepper, 1 1/2 Tbsp. butter (melted), 1 1/2 Tbsp. bread crumbs
1. Drain the cabbage well.
2. Saute onions in butter with salt and pepper until translucent.
3. Use food processor to combine cabbage and cottage cheese. Add onions.

Dough:
1 egg, 3 1/4 cups flour, salt, 1/2 cup water
1. Mix egg, flour, a little salt, and enough water for a smooth dough. Knead.
2. Roll out as thinly as possible. Cut in 3" squares.
3. Put stuffing in each square, fold into a triangle, and pinch together.
4. Cook for 5 minutes in boiling salted water.
5. Sauté bread crumbs in melted butter. Serve over the cooked pierogi.

Pierogi with Cheese

Ingredients:
1 lb. dry cottage cheese or farmer's cheese (ground), 1 egg yolk, salt, 1 1/2 Tbsp. butter, melted
1. Combine egg yolk, salt and cheese.

Dough:
1 egg, 3 1/4 cups flour, salt, 1/2 cup water
1. Mix egg, flour, a little salt, and enough water for a smooth dough. Knead.
2. Roll out as thinly as possible. Cut in 3" squares.
3. Put stuffing in each square, fold into a triangle and pinch together.
4. Cook for 5 minutes in boiling salted water.
5. Pour melted butter over pierogi.

Pierogi with Sweet Cheese

Ingredients:
1 lb. farmer's cheese, ground or ricotta cheese, 1 tsp. vanilla, 2 Tbsp. sugar, 1 egg yolk
1. Mix ingredients.

Dough:
3 1/4 cups flour, 1 egg, salt, 1/2 cup water
1. Combine flour, egg, salt, and enough water for a smooth dough. Knead.
2. Roll out as thinly as possible. Cut in 3" squares.
3. Put stuffing in each square, fold into a triangle and pinch together.
4. Cook for 5 minutes in boiling salted water.

Topping:
1 cup sour cream, 1 Tbsp. melted butter, 1/2 cup powdered sugar
1. Beat together sour cream and sugar.
2. Pour melted butter over the pierogi. Serve with the topping.

Apple Dumplings

Dough:
3 1/4 cups flour, 1 egg, salt, 1/2 cup water
1. Combine flour, egg, salt, and enough water for a smooth dough. Knead.
2. Roll out 1/4" thick on a lightly floured surface. Cut small circles.

Ingredients:
1/2 lb. apples, peeled and cored, 1 1/2 Tbsp. butter, 1 1/2 Tbsp. bread crumbs, 1/3 cup powdered sugar
1. Cut apples into small pieces.
2. Place piece of apple in middle of each dough circle and fold. Pinch edges together and roll.
3. Cook for 5 minutes in boiling salted water.
4. Combine other ingredients for apple dumpling topping.

Babka

Ingredients:

1/3 cup butter, 3/4 cup sugar, 4 eggs, 1/2 cup milk, 1/2 tsp. almond extract, 1 tsp. vanilla, 1 1/2 cups flour, 2 tsp. baking powder, bread crumbs

1. Preheat oven at 375°.
2. Cream the butter with the sugar.
3. Beat in the eggs, one by one, at high speed.
4. Beat in milk, almond extract and vanilla for 3 minutes.
5. Add dry ingredients and continue beating for 5 minutes.
6. Sprinkle well-buttered baking dish with bread crumbs, add batter and bake for 50 minutes.

Chrusciki (Angel Wings)

Ingredients:

1 dozen egg yolks, 1/4 tsp. salt, 2 Tbsp. powdered sugar, 2 Tbsp. rum extract, 1 tsp. vanilla, flour, sour cream (optional)

Optional: add 1/4 cup sour cream and 1/4 Tbsp. powdered sugar to dough

1. Beat egg yolks until lemon colored.
2. Add all ingredients except flour and sour cream.
3. Sift flour and add a little at a time until it looks like pie dough. If it gets too thick, add sour cream.
4. Roll the dough thin. Cut the dough into a diamond shape and make a slit in the middle.
5. Take one end and pull it through the slit.
6. Deep fry in hot oil (not too hot or it will burn).
7. With a fork, remove each angel wing from oil and set on paper toweling.
8. Remove to platter; sprinkle with powdered sugar.

Gołabki (Polish Cabbage Rolls)

Ingredients:

1 cabbage, large head, 1/2 lb. ground turkey, 1/2 lb. ground pork, 1 cup rice, 1 egg, 1 package of onion soup mix, 1 cup ketchup or 1 can tomato soup*,1 cup water

*Variation: cream of mushroom soup

1. Soften cabbage in microwave (or soften in boiling water in large pot).
2. Mix ground turkey and ground pork with rice, egg, and soup mix.
3. Separate cabbage leaves
4. Trim off any hard veins in order to easily roll the leaves.
5. Spoon an adequate amount of meat mixture into cabbage leaf.
6. Roll leaf forward; tuck in left and right sides; wrap with remaining side.
7. Place cabbage rolls in baking dish. Add ketchup and water.
8. Add potatoes and carrots.
9. Bake uncovered at 400° for 1 hour. Reduce temperature to 350°.
10. Cover baking dish and bake for 30 minutes or until desired tenderness is reached.

Kapusta & Kielbasa

Ingredients:

1 small head of cabbage, 1 onion, 1 can of sauerkraut, pepper

1. Chop cabbage; drain sauerkraut.
2. Sauté onion in margarine. Add sauerkraut and cabbage.
3. Cook until cabbage is tender.
4. Season with pepper.
5. Serve with Polish kielbasa (sausage).

Activities

1. Familiarize the children with the map of Poland, the location of the cities, the mountains, and the sea. Review the Polish pronunciation of the names of these places. Some maps will have Kraków spelled as Cracow and Tatry Mountains spelled as Tatra. These are their English spellings. Point out on the map the approximate locations of the three places to visit in the song *A Visit to Poland* (page 145), as written in the word list definitions.

2. The local librarian will assist you in finding audio cassettes of famous Polish composers. Ask for recordings of the music of Chopin, Paderewski, and Rubinstein. As you play the cassettes for the class, ask the students to imagine pictures or scenes that the music provokes. Request that they write a short paragraph or discuss what they imagined, heard, or felt.

3. Teach the Polish numbers by singing only one verse of *One is Jeden* each day so that the children can learn the Polish sounds a little at a time. Show them the spelling of the numbers on the number cards you have made after they have learned the sounds.

4. The various ways to decorate eggs are the theme of the song *Pisanki* (page 146). Have the children try different methods based on these Polish traditions. Eggs can be hard-boiled or hollow. Using natural items to dye eggs will show the children the different colors from dyes made from beet tops, onion skins, spinach, sunflower seeds, blackberries, and walnut shells. The color becomes darker the longer the eggs soak in the dye. Designs can be drawn on egg shells with paint colors and colored markers. Glue can be brushed on and numerous colorful items pressed on, such as paper cuttings, yarn, straw, string, and colored cutouts. Other alternatives for these painting and gluing projects are wooden, styrofoam, or plastic eggs.

5. Read the story *Rechenka's Eggs* to the class. It is a children's story about a Russian woman who paints eggs to compete in the annual Easter festival in Moscow. Invite a person who designs or collects eggs to show the students a variety of designs.

6. Paper cuttings, **wycinanki**, were very popular in Poland in the 19th century and the first part of the 20th century. Colored paper was cut with sheep shears. These cuttings were pasted on white walls or ceiling beams as home decorating, or mounted. As a folk craft, they were mounted on heavy paper. Cuttings were often items of nature. Children can create their own designs or use the pattern on page 157.

7. Locate pictures of traditional Polish costumes in libraries. *Polish Folk Costumes* by Christopher Majka and Sheilagh Hunt is a book that shows the traditional costumes and the location of the region in Poland where the dances originated.

8. Students can glue copies of the Polish dancers (pages 158-159) onto card stock. Then they can color, cut, add fasteners, and attach to dowel rods or plastic straws. They can have their Polish dancers swing their legs to the refrain of the song *The Polka*.

19 The Polish dancing puppets (pages 158-159) can also be used while singing the song *Polish Dances*. The boys and girls can sing alternating verses as indicated.

10. Borrow cassette tapes of Polish dance music such as the polka, mazurek and the oberek. The children listen and clap their hands to the rhythm of the songs.

11. Have a Polish cooking day. Ask parents to come in and help make pierogi and chrusciki with the students. With supervision, care, and a few electric skillets, the task is not difficult and produces tasty results. Serve the pierogi with sour cream and salt. Sprinkle powdered sugar on the chrusciki.

12. The Polish people are known for their hospitality and their enjoyment of food and dance. Have a Polish festival with Polish food and dance. Ask for items from Poland for display. Kielbasa, gołabki, and pierogi are sold at most grocery stores. Jelly doughnuts can substitute for the rich jelly-filled pączki. Sing the songs in the chapter. Play lively Polish dance music. Find a volunteer to teach the polka.

13. Pączki Day is the same day as Mardi Gras. On that day some stores bake pączki which are very rich doughnuts. These or regular jelly donuts can be served as a snack on Pączki Day while Polish music is played in the background.

14. Dramatize the Polish song *Marysiu* (page 148-149) on the flannel or magnetic board. The words can be sung in English as well as in Polish. Color, laminate, and cut out the figures and items. Put magnetic or felt tape on the backs of each piece and place onto the board at the appropriate time in the song. For a more lively dramatization, tape Maciek and Marysiu onto large craft sticks and use them as stick puppets.

15. Write or telephone the Polish Embassy for more information, pamphlets, and brochures: Consulate General of the Republic of Poland, 233 Madison Avenue, New York, NY 10016, Telephone (212) 889-8360 1/2/3 or Embassy of the Republic of Poland, 2640 16th Street, NW, Washington, DC 20036, Telephone (202) 483-3800, 3801, 3802.

BOOKS TO READ

The Creche of Kraków
Harvey and Audrey Hirsch
Fifty years after fleeing war-torn Poland, Grandma Anne receives a gift from the past

Bochek in Poland
Joseph Contoski
A children's story about the fairy tale birds of the old world

The Glass Mountain
W.S. Kuniczak
Twenty-six ancient Polish folktalkes and fables

Polish Folk Tales
translated by Lucia Borski
A collection of sixteen folk tales

Tales of Early Poland
Sigmund Uminski
A collection of twelve Polish legends dating back to the ninth century

Treasured Polish Folk Rhymes, Songs and Games
translated by the Polanie Editorial Staff
Old Polish rhymes and games in Polish and English

Reunion in Poland
Jean Karsavina
The story of two teenagers living in occupied Poland during World War II

The Trumpeter of Kraków
Eric P. Kelly
The commemoration of a brave act in ancient Krakow saves lives two centuries later

STASIU

158

ZOSIA

159

PATTERNS

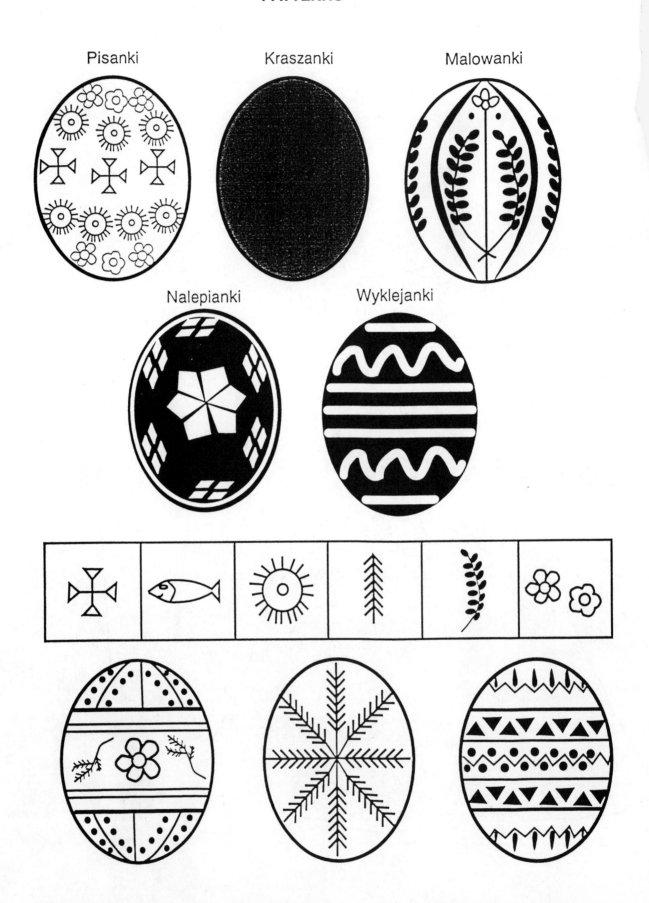

Pisanki

Kraszanki

Malowanki

Nalepianki

Wyklejanki